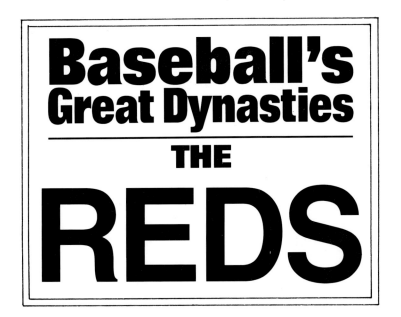

Baseball's Great Dynasties
THE
REDS

Baseball's Great Dynasties
THE
REDS

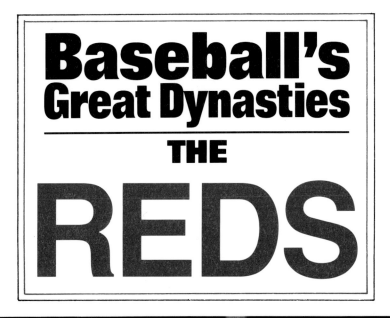

Peter C. Bjarkman

GALLERY BOOKS
An imprint of W.H. Smith Publishers Inc.
112 Madison Avenue
New York, New York 10016

For Bill Friday, my bullpen ace

Published by Gallery Books
A Division of W.H. Smith Publishers Inc.
112 Madison Avenue
New York, New York 10016

Produced by
Brompton Books Corp.
15 Sherwood Place
Greenwich, CT 06830

ISBN 0-8317-0626-0

Printed in Hong Kong

10 9 8 7 6 5 4 3 2 1

PICTURE CREDITS

All photos courtesy of UPI/Bettmann Newsphotos
 except the following:
Dwayne LaBakas: 50(bottom), 51(both), 52(bottom),
 53(top), 54, 56, 57(bottom), 58(both), 59(both), 61,
 63(top), 64(bottom), 66(both).
National Baseball Library, Cooperstown, NY: 8, 10,
 12, 14, 18, 21, 22, 24, 25, 26, 27(right), 29(bottom),
 30, 31(both), 32, 33(both), 35(top left), 40(right),
 48(bottom).
Ponzini Photography: 6, 57(top), 60, 64(top),
 67(both), 69(all four), 70, 71(both), 72(both),
 73(left), 77(top right).
Bruce Schwartzman: 73(right), 75(middle).

ACKNOWLEDGMENTS

The author and publisher would like to thank the
following people who helped in the preparation of
this book: Rita Longabucco, the picture editor; Don
Longabucco, the designer; Jean Martin, the editor;
and Elizabeth McCarthy, the indexer.

Page 1: *Baseball's "all-time greatest" catcher Johnny Bench applies his patented "sweeping tag" against Oakland runner Dick Green in 1972 World Series Game 2 action.*

Page 2: *The Reds opened a new decade of the 1990s led by a young stable of star batsmen including heavy-hitting shortstop Barry Larkin.*

Page 3: *The most celebrated moment in Reds history: Pete Rose rides atop the shoulders of Tony Perez and Dave Concepcion after breaking Ty Cobb's long-standing hits record.*

This page: *The original "Nasty Boys" – Milt Wilcox, Clay Carroll, Wayne Granger, and Don Gullett – pose before 1970 World Series action with the Baltimore Orioles.*

Contents

Preface

They may not have always been baseball's greatest team, but from the very outset the Cincinnati professional baseball club has always been intimately bonded to the best and the worst of baseball's glorious traditions. Not only the sport's oldest franchise, it is also the National League team with an unparalleled hold on some of baseball's most memorable historic moments.

Professional baseball as we know it today actually began with Harry Wright's touring Red Stockings outfit of 1869. The earliest decades of National League play in the nineteenth-century were always represented by a Queen City entry, if not always a very good one. Some of the most colorful players of the game's earliest days – Wahoo Sam Crawford, Noodles Hahn, Edd Roush – also performed at the Palace of Fans in quaint nineteenth-century Cincinnati. And what other team has been so frequently involved in some of the game's highest and lowest moments? This was the "other team" – the forgotten winner – in the shameful 1919 Black Sox scandal that nearly sent the national pastime to an early demise. This was the team that hosted the game's greatest single pitching performance, back-to-back no-hitters by unheralded yet now immortal Johnny Vander Meer. This is the team whose fans were once so fanatic as to cram the ballot box and elect an entire roster of Redlegs stars to the 1957 National League All-Star team. No dynasty has ever been so potent or dominating over a short span as that menacing Big

Johnny Bench was the tireless engine who drove the awesome Big Red Machine. Teammate Pete Rose flashed the hustle and often took the headlines, but Bench supplied the power and often drove home the victories. Today Rose waits along the sidelines for his transgressions to be forgiven and his reputation to be fully sanctified in Cooperstown, while Bench has taken his proper and well-deserved place in Baseball's Hall of Fame. Few experts would dispute that he was the greatest catcher ever to strap on the "tools of ignorance" throughout the long history of the national pastime.

Reds' 1990 Series slugging hero Chris Sabo (foreground with glasses) and clutch-hitting catcher Joe Oliver (top) – the hero of Game 2 – join a joyous celebration in Oakland's Coliseum as the Reds rush onto the field after the final pitch of a 2-1 Game 4 win over the heavily favored American League champion Oakland A's. Most experts agreed that it would be a four-game sweep in 1990, but few of baseball's soothsayers had predicted victory for the underrated "Little Red Machine" ballclub of first-year manager Lou Piniella. The 1990 World Series victory was indeed one of the sweetest in the long history of Cincinnati Reds National League baseball.

Red Machine team which arose in the new stadium on the banks of the Ohio River during the first half of the 1970s. And no baseball event of the modern age has so captured the national attention or created more passionate fervor than did Pete Rose's dramatic chase of Ty Cobb's seemingly unreachable career record for base hits which culminated in Cincinnati at the close of the 1985 season. But above all else – for history and ceremony – Opening Day in Cincinnati's Crosley Field and Riverfront Stadium has become a national tradition at the heart of baseball legend and lore.

As bound as the Reds are to some of baseball's most noble traditions – being the game's oldest and one of its most storied franchises – the baseball team from Cincinnati has from the start also been the national pastime's most celebrated trail-blazer. No other major league club can boast the long string of "firsts" which mark the history of Cincinnati baseball: the first professional franchise, the first ballclub to hold a Ladies Day, the first to option players to the minor leagues and the first to maintain a legitimate farm system, the first to travel by air, the first to host big-league night baseball, and the first to televise a championship season game. At the outset of baseball's modern television era in the 1970s, the Reds pioneered the flight of major league clubs from decaying urban ballparks of an earlier epoch into modern downtown multipurpose stadia stamped with the synthetic image of the streamlined television game. Thus the Reds of Cincinnati also stood at the forefront of a new tradition: linking baseball progress with inner city pride and with the downtown rede-

Paul Derringer teamed with Bucky Walters in the pennant-winning years of 1939 and 1940 to form the finest one-two mound punch in Cincinnati club history. When the Reds copped their first flag in 20 long years in 1939, the hard-throwing right-hander was second in the league to teammate Walters in victories (25), innings pitched (301), and complete games (28), while pacing the circuit in winning percentage (.781) and fewest walks allowed per nine innings (1.05). The finest summer of his successful 15-year career (223-112) was sandwiched between campaigns in which he also won 21 (1938) and 20 (1940). Derringer also holds the club single-season record for losses, however, with 25 in 1933.

velopment programs necessary in the early 1970s to preserve some of America's oldest and proudest urban centers.

Baseball in Cincinnati remains an irrepressible link to the game's well-established nineteenth-century heritage. This blue collar city on the shores of the Ohio River has taken its identity from its professional ballclub perhaps more exclusively than any other metropolis in history. Opening Day of the new baseball season remains the major civic event on Cincinnati's annual social calendar, a fact which remains as true in the seemingly tradition-less 1990s as it was in the pre-television age of radio baseball. The "Pete Rose Affair" which so troubled the baseball world throughout the late summer of 1989 was this entire city's exclusive and ubiquitous political and social passion – an issue of endless radio talk-show debate and heated public emotions – as it dragged on for months and inevitably grew to be wearisome "old news" in other cities across the land. And nowhere is baseball tradition still more alive and fermenting than in the city which gave the nation its first taste of night baseball, daily radio baseball, commercial televised baseball, the prototype contemporary artificial playing field and almost every other important diamond innovation conceivable. Cincinnati's Reds today reign, without doubt or dispute, as the ballclub infused with the most indelible baseball tradition. They stand alone and unrivalled as the oldest, proudest, and most storied national franchise in all of American sports history.

Left: *Bobby Tolan crosses the plate after hitting an eighth-inning home run over the right field barrier during a 1970 contest in the Houston Astrodome. Big Red Machine slugger Tony Perez (24) awaits Tolan at the plate to offer congratulations. Tolan, whose unique batting style featured the bat held high above his head and perpendicular to the ground, enjoyed brilliant seasons in 1969 and 1970.*

Below: *Elio Chacon slides home with a fifth-inning Redlegs' run during Game 2 of the 1961 World Series in Yankee Stadium.*

1. Cincinnati's Colorful Hometown Game

Above all else, Cincinnati's beloved hometown Reds are baseball's champions of innovation. Infrequently has a ballclub representing the city of Cincinnati stood first in the National League standings – only three pennants have been won there in over a century of play that preceded the glorious Big Red Machine teams of the mid-1970s. It is Cincinnati baseball alone, however, that has witnessed such pioneering moments as the nation's first professional team (1869); baseball's first rainout (ironically in the first official Red Stockings game scheduled against the Antioch nine on May 31, 1869); the first uniformed manager (Harry Wright in 1869); the first fielder's glove (donned by Red Stockings catcher Douglas Allison in 1869); and catcher's mitt (devised by Harry Decker in 1890); even the first double play (recorded by Fred Waterman in 1869 against the New York Mutuals). When fresh baseball ground has been broken, it has almost always been in the River City of Cincinnati.

Cincinnati's special penchant for baseball pioneering has ranged over the years from the truly momentous to the downright trivial: the first-ever seventh-inning stretch (1869) and baseball's first beat writer (Harry Millar in 1869); the advent of spring training (1870); the sport's first switch-hitter (Bob Ferguson, in the famous 1870 game against the Brooklyn Atlantics, when the invincible Cincinnati nine tasted their first defeat in 130 incredible outings), first doubleheader (1876), and first no-hitter (1876, against the Red Stockings by Boston's Joe Borden). The first home run in National League history involved the Cincy ballclub (slugged by Chicago's Ross Barnes on May 2, 1876, to be followed with one by Cincinnati's Charley Jones in the same contest), as did the league's inaugural lefthanded pitcher (Bobby Mitchell in 1877). The invention of the catcher's squat

The original Red Stockings of 1869 were baseball's first professional team and consisted of but one player for each position on the original "ironman" nine. From left to right, with their positions and non-sporting professions: Captain Harry Wright (CF, jeweler); Asa Brainard (P, insurance); Charles Gould (1B, bookkeeper); Fred A. Waterman (3B, insurance); Charles Sweasy (2B, hatter); Andy Leonard (LF, hatter); Calvin McVey (RF, pianomaker); Doug Allison (C, marblecutter); and George Wright (SS, engraver).

(Buck Ewing in 1880) and the debut of uniform numbers (briefly in 1883) are also long-lost Cincinnati baseball credits. Cincinnati was home as well to an unprecedented ambidextrous pitcher (Tony Mullane in 1886) and a lefthanded third baseman (Hick Carpenter in 1879); the first Ladies Day (1886); the first farm system (1887, with a working agreement between the Cincinnati American Association ballclub and a minor league team in Emporia, Kansas); the first sale of season's tickets (1934); the first time ever posting of "errors," upon the Crosley Field scoreboard (1934); the first air travel by a big league ballclub (1934); the inauguration of big league night baseball (occurring at Crosley Field on May 24, 1935); the first televised league game (involving Cincinnati at Brooklyn on August 26, 1939); and the very first all-synthetic playing surface, in present-day Riverfront Stadium (1970).

Blended with this spirit of radical innovation – altogether rare in a sport so known for its conservatism – is the Cincinnati ballclub's longstanding sense of baseball tradition. Cincinnati is, after all, the city where professional baseball first began in 1869, and it remains today's proud home to the annual spring rite of baseball's richly ceremonial Opening Day. Throughout the past

century and a quarter this venerable baseball franchise, which fittingly debuted in the National League in 1876 as a charter member of baseball's senior circuit, has also been home to some of the game's greatest moments and some of its most colorful players. In fact, no two single players in the game's entire history have ever been as unbendingly revered by the adoring hometown fans as have lead-footed yet free-swinging catcher Ernie Lombardi who enlivened the lackluster 1930s pre-war Reds, and homegrown hero Pete Rose ("Charlie Hustle"), the fire and spirit behind the modern-day Big Red Machine, baseball's dominant team in National League play of the early and mid-1970s.

The factors which link baseball tradition and innovation in the Queen City are all-pervasive. Cincinnati baseball historians Lonnie Wheeler and John Baskin have even suggested (in their excellent 1988 coffee table history, *The Cincinnati Game*) that the city's modern-day baseball folk hero, Pete Rose, would have been altogether at home managing that original Red Stockings outfit of Harry Wright which pioneered organized baseball during the immediate post-Civil War years. Somehow the thought of Pete Rose – baseball's true prodigal son of the 1990s – linked with the

In a city of diamond landmarks and milestones, none was more significant for the major league game than the innovation of night baseball. A crowd of 20,422 was on hand as President Roosevelt threw a switch in Washington and illuminated the field for the first big league night game on May 24, 1935 in Crosley Field. Paul Derringer threw the first pitch and the Reds triumphed over the Phillies 2-1. Some 632 lamps were used to light the ballpark still known at the time as Redland Field. The event was scheduled for a night earlier, but had been washed out by rainfall.

Deacon Bill McKechnie was a soft-spoken and fatherly leader who earned an honored space in Cincinnati baseball history by leading the pennant-hungry Reds to two consecutive titles in 1939 and 1940. Deacon Bill was a prototype of the classic "book" manager and specialist in fine defensive ballclubs. McKechnie still ranks ninth on the all-time managerial win list (with 1898 victories) and is to date the only skipper to pilot three different ballclubs (Pittsburgh, Cincinnati, and St. Louis) in World Series play.

pantalooned cricket players that were the Cincinnati Red Stockings of 1869 – America's first professional barnstorming baseball team – at first seems to defy both common sense and the most fertile of imaginations. Yet there is something quite alluring about the prospect. As Wheeler and Baskin suggest, Rose and the Red Stockings of Harry Wright would have been a more comfortable match than two distinct centuries might at first encompass. For there is a seemingly inevitable link between the knicker-clad pioneers who first brought sporting fame to the Queen City (especially given their "rough-and-tumble" style of play and businesslike approach to winning) and the hard-nosed tradition-breaker who, a full century and a quarter later, would become both baseball's much-glorified all-time hitting champion and its most embarrassing "bad boy" outcast, virtually at one and the same time. "They were his kind of men," observe Wheeler and Baskin, commenting on Rose's assumed attitudes about the hard-playing, fast-living (and certainly free-wagering) men of Harry Wright's original pioneering Cincinnati nine.

Part of Cincinnati's special link with baseball's past rests in its status as the national pastime's oldest and first baseball city – the original and unprecedented pioneer in the evolutionary growth of the nation's foremost spectator sport. Yet throughout the past century and a quarter this city on the banks of the Ohio River, nestled between the farm states of Ohio, Indiana and Kentucky, has also been home to some of the game's greatest moments and most colorful players. Cincinnati baseball memories are legion and irrepressible. There is the still-vivid sight of ungainly Ewell Blackwell in the immediate post-war years, mowing down hitters with his whip-lash sidewinder delivery and crafting a memorable no-hitter against the Boston Braves. There is the lasting image of Bill McKechnie, the team's greatest manager, carrying on his own wartime tactics in the 1940s against the league's embattled umpires. There is also the unforgettable portrait of Johnny Ripple racing across home plate with the winning run of the 1940 World Series against Detroit; of Paul Derringer staggering to a pennant-clinching victory against the Cardinals at the eleventh hour of the 1939 campaign; of Ernie Lombardi pawing the dirt behind home plate and terrorizing the league's pitchers during baseball's Golden Decade of the 1930s. Above all else, there is the undying memory of that young and unheralded New Jersey strongboy, Johnny Vander Meer, weaving baseball legend with his yet-unparalleled feat of two consecutive no-hit performances. And there is the heavy artillery fleet of long-ball sluggers led by muscle-bound Ted Kluszewski blasting out a league-record onslaught of prodigious homers in the mid-1950s.

Daydreams of an earlier era still conjure up the immortal portrait of incomparable center fielder Edd Roush lashing out countless hits and lunging for countless spear-like catches in the deep recesses of Crosley Field's distant outfield pastures; of Fred Toney matching up with Chicago's Hippo Vaughn during the memorable summer of 1917 to craft baseball's only double no-hit game ever witnessed during the sport's full century of modern play; of immortal Christy Mathewson making his single memorable pitching appearance in Reds colors during a classic matchup with his arch foe, Three Finger Brown; and of Cy Seymour splashing base hits across National League fields during his team-record .377 batting season of 1905. And at the game's dawn in the previous century there is the rare memory of Bid McPhee ending his hold-out in 1896 as the last big league fielder without a glove; of Tony Mullane pitching to befuddled batters with either arm in the 1886 through 1893 seasons (the only hurler to be listed in the *Baseball Encyclopedia* with the odd distinction of "BB" and "TB", indicating switch-pitching as well as switch-hitting!). And finally, there are dusty ferrotype images of the original Red Stockings under Harry and George Wright, barnstorming cross-country to 130 consecutive victories against all comers in two summers of play.

Storied players have, in fact, worn the Cincinnati flannels in every generation and throughout every decade of past baseball play. Buck Ewing and Bid McPhee were incomparable stars of the nineteenth century: The former revolutionized play as a catcher, batsman and manager, while the latter was hailed in the pioneer diamond days as the "king bee of second basemen" and held the franchise record for career hits (2249) until Pete Rose came along. Wahoo Sam Crawford and Edd Roush had few peers as both hitters and fielders in the National League outfields of the current century's first two decades. Bucky Walters and Paul Derringer were as fearsome a pitching duo (jointly winning 52 games in the first pennant year of 1939 and 42 the next) as National League hitters would see in the immediate pre-World War II years. The "Big Stick" hitters of the 1950s – Kluszewski, Post, Bell, Bailey and Robinson – rewrote ancient baseball records and formed lasting legends; and even if they were to bring altogether few victories and no pennants to tiny Crosley Field, they were nonetheless to brutalize the league's pitchers in tandem onslaught for five glorious summers, when Elvis Presley was still a novelty and rock-and-roll the newest

Left: *Ted Kluszewski was reputed to be the strongest man in baseball, and if this was not easy to document, it was certainly easy enough to conclude from pictures like this classic 1950 pose in Crosley Field. A lifetime .300 hitter until his last season in LA, Big Klu was a fine hitter whose overall batting skills were belied by his reputation for brute power. He was also one of the finest glovemen at his position in the league. Klu's early-season run at Ruth's record of 60 roundtrippers in 1954 (he ended with a league-best 49) went far to foster a reputation for fence-busting strength which overshadowed the overall skill of the National League's best first sacker of the early 1950s.*

national craze. Finally, the original Big Red Machine of the early 1970s – Bench, Morgan, Perez and Rose – was arguably the most dominant single team in National League history, save only the Boys of Summer Dodgers of the Jackie Robinson-Branch Rickey era.

Cincinnati has also remained home to unusual and nostalgic diamond events, often of the strangest and most unprecedented order. Most memorable was the remarkable "double no-hitter" of 1917, the only game of its kind ever to occur in big-league play. Cincinnati's Fred Toney won this unique matchup with 10 innings of hitless magic, while his ill-starred mound opponent, the Cubs' Jim Vaughn, himself wove nine hitless innings before surrendering two hits and victory in the fateful tenth

Far left: *Paul Derringer was noted for his trademark high-kicking delivery and four years as a 20-game winner while in a Redlegs uniform. Yet in 1933, the first year he pulled on the Reds' colors, Derringer lost a league-high 27 contests, two with the Cardinals and the rest with struggling last-place Cincy.*

frame. While this greatest pitching duel in baseball history was actually staged at Chicago's Weeghman Park, it was a Cincinnati stalwart who served as central player in what remains baseball's most unusual pitching moment. There were as well the back-to-back no-hitters of Cincinnati's Johnny Vander Meer, this time transpiring in June 1938 at Crosley Field and (four days later) at Brooklyn's Ebbets Field, the latter record-shattering affair ironically being the first night game in New York baseball history. And since history-making no-hit performances seem to be a special Cincinnati entertainment, there was the April 1964 game in Houston in which Astros hurler Ken Johnson became the first moundsman (and only one, until Andy Hawkins of the Yankees joined this select club in 1990) to toss a nine-inning no-hitter and actually lose, being victimized 1-0 by the opportunistic Redlegs. And if this were not all

*Between the World Series heroics of hurler Bucky Walters (**Opposite**), who won two Series games in 1940 after dropping two the previous fall, and slugger Frank Robinson (**Left**), whose summertime marks of 37 homers and 124 RBIs did not hold up against New York Yankee pitching in the 1961 Classic, quaint Crosley Field (**Below**) saw no World Series action and few serious pennant runs by the hometown Reds.*

They were known as "The Big Red Machine," and that designation today is rivalled among colorful baseball nicknames only by "Murderers' Row" as a symbol of pure fence-busting offense. On the eve of the 1970 World Series opener in new Riverfront Stadium, Red Machine stalwarts here pose on a farm tractor with their trusty lumber: (L to R) Bobby Tolan, Johnny Bench, Tony Perez, Lee Maye and Pete Rose. It is fitting, of course, that the team's heart and soul – Johnny Bench – should be in the driver's seat of this miniature Big Red Machine.

enough, the Reds' own Jim Maloney would, the very next season, himself become the only pitcher in all of baseball's long and glorious history to toss two extra-inning no-hitters (one of which he managed to lose), opportunistically cramming his two rare masterpieces together into the same action-packed summer.

In the modern age, the Reds have also maintained their long-standing franchise penchant for both uncompromising baseball tradition and unparalleled baseball innovation. Over the course of the past two decades the Cincinnati ballclub has represented better than any present-day club, save perhaps the Cardinals in St. Louis, the vital link between baseball's evolution and the proud revitalization of America's downtown urban centers. A shift in 1970 from neighborhood-friendly yet decaying Crosley Field to sterile, carpeted and waterside Riverfront Stadium was admittedly a calculated showpiece in the city's onslaught on urban blight and its game plan for downtown civic rejuvenation and inner city renaissance. At the same time, the Cincinnati ballclub has repeatedly touted deep-rooted formal connections with baseball tradition, especially during the era of the Big Red Machine under the administration of general manager Bob Howsam. Clean-shaven ballplayers, shiny white flannels (with uniform black shoes and old-style high socks), and absolute uniformity of team appearance demanded by Howsam were not only a rejection of the gaudy uniforms, unkempt appearance and showy displays of individual uniform variation which were the trademark of such other modern-day teams as the Oakland Athletics of Charlie O. Finley; they were also part and parcel of a carefully orchestrated corporate masterplan to market longstanding commitments by the Cincinnati National League franchise to baseball's most cherished and sustaining old-time traditions.

And Cincinnati's modern-era Reds, down to the present hour, have maintained a trademark local tradition of colorful and controversial players as well. No single athlete fits this bill in the present decade more than Pete Rose, baseball's prototypical modern-day bad boy and the very epitome for baseball fans everywhere of ceaseless hustle and win-at-all-costs play. But there have been other colorful Queen City diamond characters down through the lean years and the glory years. The supply, in fact, is almost limitless: Dolf Luque, baseball's first Latin American star, charging from the mound in the heat of play to flatten heckling Casey Stengel on the Giants bench in an infamous 1922 incident, fashioning the single finest Reds mound performance in history (27-8, 1.93 ERA in

1922), and pioneering as the first Latin pitcher in post-season play during the celebrated 1919 Black Sox Series; Ted Kluszewski, rippling his huge biceps under the sleeveless jerseys he inspired for the 1950s Redlegs, crushing mammoth Crosley Field home runs, yet also surprisingly leading National League first basemen in fielding a major-league-record five consecutive seasons; Dummy Hoy, baseball's greatest deaf player who reputedly inspired the umpire's hand signals and undisputedly banged out enough base hits (2054) and demonstrated sufficient baserunning and fielding skills in four different leagues at the turn of the century to stand as a legitimate Hall of Fame candidate in his own right; Ewell

Blackwell, possessor of baseball's most celebrated and unusual pitching delivery; gigantic Ernie Lombardi, owner of the game's slowest pair of feet and yet one of its most fearsome and heavy bats as well; and Noodles Hahn, an incomparable fastballer of the "dead ball era" who for six years (1899-1904) outranked such contemporary Hall of Fame moundsmen as Jack Chesboro, Cy Young, Rube Waddell and Christy Mathewson. Each of these rare and colorful Cincinnati baseball legends, along with dozens more chronicled in the following pages, has contributed in unique ways to what is now an indelible part of American sports history – the story of Cincinnati's own special hometown hardball game.

With their 1990 entry in the Fall Classic, the Reds have shown their stuff nine times in World Series play and won the coveted World Title on four occasions. None was more surprising and more significant than the very first – the Reds' shocking triumph in the tainted best-of-nine Series of 1919. Here captains Eddie Collins of Chicago and Heinie Groh of Cincinnati exchange the customary handshake before the opener of the 1919 "Black Sox" Series at Redland Field. Few today remember that the underdog Reds – Series winner by the margin of 5-3 – had actually won eight more regular season games than Comiskey's White Sox and had breezed to a most comfortable nine-game margin of victory in the NL race.

2. The Red Stockings' Original Nineteenth-Century Game

Young Harry Wright and his brothers arrived in America with their father, a foremost English cricket player hired by the New York St. George cricket club, but the young Wright soon took a fancy to the new American form of "rounders." Harry first played with New York's successful Knickerbocker club, and then was hired on by Cincinnati city fathers who decided that a winning baseball club might put their town on the map. Wright remained in Cincinnati for but two years before managing the Boston Red Stockings after 1871 in the new National Association, but his undefeated 1869 Cincy ballteam spread the popularity of baseball with its successful 65-game national tour.

From the outset Cincinnati has worked hard to carve out its well-earned reputation as the national pastime's most persistent pioneer. In the earliest years, however, triumphs were often only temporary and a permanent place in baseball history for the city's sporting heritage was never very solidly assured. In fact, Cincinnati's spectacular impact on the founding of the professional game had been of only the most fleeting duration. Harry Wright's barnstorming Red Stockings of 1869-70 were hastily disbanded after only a second season of play, once hoopla surrounding the club's fabulous unbeaten streak sagged (along with attendance at the games) on the heels of four defeats at the tail end of a second campaign. Wright's experiment had launched such burgeoning popularity for the game, however, that a full-fledged league was almost immediately formed under the name of the National Association in 1871. Harry Wright himself simply moved his baseball operation lock, stock and barrel into Boston, where he took over operation of a regrouped Red Stockings ballclub (forefather of the modern Red Sox) in this newly minted professional league. The city of Cincinnati, on the other hand, would have to wait five more summers for the rival National League to come along before it was once more back in the baseball business.

When the time-honored National League was christened some 115 summers ago, baseball's original pioneer city was, of course, there to be tallied as a respected charter member. The first decade of National League play was far from glorious, however, for the midwestern team still wearing red stockings and already boasting a distinguished if short-lived baseball heritage. The opening campaign, in fact, saw the Red Stockings post a record of futility which has not even been approximated in the long century-plus history of big-league action which has followed. Cincinnati's first baseball owner, Josiah Keck, seemingly displayed impeccable judgement in hiring as his first manager the only homegrown Cincinnatian to have played with the original roving Red Stockings under Harry Wright. But local hero Charlie Gould proved anything but up to the task, as his inaugural club achieved infamy by becoming the only professional team ever to win fewer than double-digits for an entire season. With but nine wins and a season's .138 victory percentage, Gould's single managerial season set a record of ineptness matched perhaps only by the 1899 Cleveland Spiders who rang up an immortal 20-134 league mark. And things didn't get very much better in much of a hurry in the nation's leading beer town either, as only the second-place 1878 team under manager Cal McVey made anything like a respectable run at the league championship trophy. If there was a single bright spot in the opening decade of National League play on the banks of the Ohio River it was the iron-man performances of bespectacled hurler Will White, who single-handedly pitched an entirely unimaginable 1148 innings in 1878-79, hurling in an astonishing 76 of his team's 78 league games (75 as a starter!) in the latter of those two years.

When the new rival league – the American Association – opened its doors for formal business in 1882, baseball's true pioneer franchise was once again there at the very head of the line. When a group of disenchanted midwestern baseball promoters, all of whom resented the National League's steadfast ban on the sordid practices of Sunday baseball and beer sales at the league's ballparks, got together under the leadership of St. Louis brewing magnate Chris von der Ahe to form their own rival league without such business-tainting policies, popular Cincinnati baseball writer Oliver P. Caylor was counted in their number. Cincinnati had just suffered

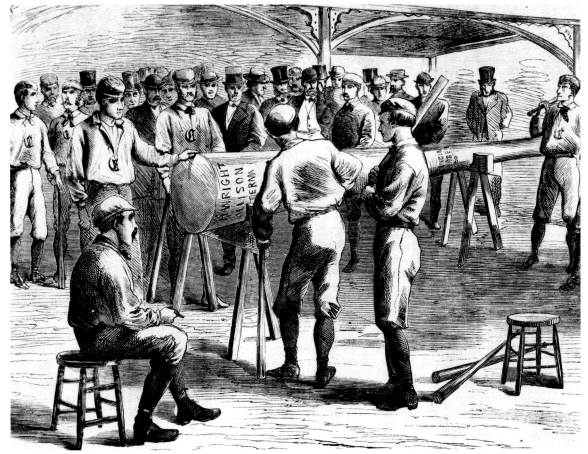

Above: *Cincinnati's first professional team was formed under the daring notion that people would actually pay to see the newly organized and wildly popular American version of "rounders" which we now know as baseball. This lithograph displays the original nine in striking formal portraits.*

Left: *An artist's popular rendition of a ceremonial presentation of a huge hand-carved champions' bat awarded to the 1869 Red Stockings at the conclusion of their successful undefeated national tour.*

Widespread public interest in the huge salaries of pro ballplayers dates to the very first year of the professional game. So popular was the original hometown "nine" in Cincinnati that salaries of the original Harry Wright Red Stockings were a matter of full public record. Reading clockwise from top left, players and their 1869 salaries are as follows: Charles H. Sweasy ($800), Harry Wright ($1200), Douglas Allison ($800), Fred A. Waterman ($1000), Calvin McVey ($800), Andrew J. Leonard ($800), Asa Brainard, pitcher and winner of all 65 games during 1869 ($1100), George Wright ($1400), and Charles Gould ($800). But such lofty salaries for that day and age were not at all an indication of a lucrative business in the new game of barnstorming baseball, as the original Red Stockings ballclub earned a profit of but $1.23 over its only two seasons of professional play.

through the 1881 campaign without any league affiliation or even any team at all, after the Reds had been suspended from National League play for their continued defiant policies of ballpark beer vending and leasing their vacant baseball grounds to amateur teams for Sunday play. The real reason for the expulsion, however, seems to have been that the crusading Caylor had convinced Reds' president William C. Kennett to petition the league bosses to drop the circuit's reserve-clause policies, contending that such contracts which restricted a player's commitment to a single franchise were both illegal and immoral. The league fathers' response was to consider the upstart Cincinnati management to be filled with dangerous radicals and to boot the club promptly right out of the league.

Once Cincinnatian Caylor joined with von der Ahe and renowned St. Louis writer Al Spink to form the new freewheeling league – which immediately announced popular beer and alcohol sales at its parks and dropped admission prices to twenty-five cents, half that of the established National League – Cincinnati baseball was back in business, and the revived franchise marked its new beginning most visibly by shortening its adopted club name from Red Stockings to simply Reds. With Kennett still in the front office, this new revival of the old hometown ballclub, with a new league to play in, also sported a startling new look. Retaining only two players from the 1880 team (pitcher Will White and third baseman Hick Carpenter), the Reds took the field under new skipper Pop Snyder with a stunning appearance that would have done Charles Finley proud: each player was brightly clad in a different color uniform – White wore blue, Snyder scarlet, barehanded rookie second sacker Bid McPhee orange and black, etc. Whether stunning their opponents with these visual effects or simply with the great pitching prowess of Will White (40-12), great defense (where they led the league with a .907 Pct. in an age not known for adept fielding play), or great hitting by Hick Carpenter (league leader with 120 hits), the Cincinnatians ran off to a 55-25 record for their best winning percentage of the decade. The result was an unchallenged 11½-game final margin over runnerup Philadelphia. This was indeed an

auspicious start, but not one to be maintained very long as the club tumbled quickly to third the following summer, despite White's second straight 40-win outing (and perhaps because of a return to more traditional baseball garb).

Eight American Association seasons were hardly successful ones for the Cincinnati nine, despite a surprising start in 1882 and a solid if not invincible club on three other occasions. The team earned respectable second-place finishes in 1885 and 1887 (though 16 games off the pace in one of those campaigns and a full 14 the other), and one third-place finish (1883) as well as a single league pennant in the inaugural season of 1882. Yet if the team won only one championship flag, it also suffered but one sub-.500 campaign, in 1886. And what was often little more than average league play was spiced up by the performances of several highly capable pitchers who wore the Cincinnati colors in those forgotten pioneer years. One Cincinnati hurler in particular, William Henry "Will" White, sported both a proud family heritage in the new hardball sport and a record of diamond accomplishment that today seems more the stuff of legend than the fallout of history.

In a brief 10-year career now all but buried in the musty archives of nineteenth-

The Red Stockings did not suffer a single loss in their maiden season, perfection being marred only by a controversial tie in Troy, New York. The first defeat came in 1870 against the Brooklyn Atlantics, after 92 consecutive documented victories. Not many of these games were played in Cincinnati, though this one rare photographic image does remain of an 1869 contest in the Union Grounds ballyard, the site where Union Terminal was later built. Note the large crowd, covered wooden grandstand, and apparent lack of catchers during play.

As an inaugural member of the new American Association, the 1882 Cincinnati Reds walked away with the first Association championship with a record of 55-25 and an 11½-game margin over the runner-up Philadelphia club. This famed club, however, is best known today for its revolutionary style of on-field dress, each member of the starting nine wearing a different bright color on his uniform flannels. Among notable players found in this snappy team portrait are left-handed third sacker Hick Carpenter (far left); manager Pop Snyder (second from left in middle row); and star pitcher Will White, who won 40 games that season and 43 in the next campaign (in center with eyeglasses).

century baseball lore, Will White accomplished the now unimaginable feat of posting back-to-back 40-win seasons in the first two summers of American Association play, a yeomanly but not unparalleled summer's work at the time. Respected baseball historian Lee Allen refers to White as "one of the game's true greats who has never received his due" from a baseball establishment which largely ignores the game's pre-turn-of-the-century roots. The first player to wear eyeglasses on the field of play, Will White is today as well-known for being the brother of Deacon White (member of both Harry Wright's first Red Stockings lineup and Cap Anson's White Stockings outfit which took the first-ever National League crown) as he is for what should more appropriately be his lasting fame – American Association standards in ERA (2.09 in 1883) and winning percentage (40-12, .769, in 1882). Author of a 40-victory season in the National League as well in 1879, White was more often than not a victim of the haplessness of his inept Cincinnati teammates,

witnessed by his 18-42 mark (in which he personally accounted for 42 percent of his ballclub's defeats) for the last place Queen City team during the 1880 National League campaign. Ambidextrous Tony Mullane (31 victories in both 1886 and 1887), southpaw Elmer Smith (33-18, with a league best 2.94 ERA in 1887) and righthander Jesse Duryea (32-19 in his rookie 1889 season) were also Cincinnati 30-game winners during this decade of the soon-to-disappear rubber-armed nineteenth-century hurler.

The "Gay Nineties" joyfully saw the Cincinnati ballclub back in the National League fold where it seemingly had belonged all along, though the largest cheers at the time probably went up in rival cities around the league, thrilled at the prospect of beating up again on the doormat Reds team. The American Association had made quick peace with the rival National League and was eventually exploited as something of a helpless pawn of the more established and wealthier circuit, whose crafty owners attempted to ward off the

booming bats of Willie Keeler and Hugh Jennings) and Cleveland (featuring batting champ Jesse Burkett, who hit a lofty .410), this 1896 Cincinnati nine boasted a first-rate outfield of Dummy Hoy, Eddie Burke and Dusty Miller, a trio who together batted a composite .314 and pilfered an astounding 179 bases.

The final decade of the outgoing century did witness some remarkable individual stars for the hometown Cincinnati ballclub, despite the endlessly mediocre team finishes spread throughout the era. It was during this decade and the one that preceded it that tiny Bid McPhee established himself as a hometown baseball institution, playing longer at second base (18 seasons) than any man for any other team before or since. An even more spritely Hugh Nicol arrived in Cincinnati from the St. Louis team in time for the 1887 American Association season and amassed 138 stolen bases, a record never to be matched in the modern age of big league play. Hick Carpenter was undoubtedly the game's greatest lefty-throwing third sacker (if admittedly the competition has remained almost nil for such an honor) though he batted above .300 but once in his dozen big league seasons. And showing a special penchant for pint-sized diamond heroes, Cincinnati was also home to a 5-foot 7-inch slugger named Bug Holliday who belted out the then-extraordinary league-leading home run totals of 19 and 13 in 1889 and 1892 respectively. Exploiting a squatty stance and the quickest swing of his era, Holliday seems from today's perspective to have been something of a rare nineteenth-century equivalent to such popular "toy cannons" of later ages as Hack Wilson, Mel Ott, Jim Wynn and Kirby Puckett.

One final figure – also huge of reputation if not lofty of physical stature – was to grace the Cincinnati baseball scene before decade's end as well. An unparalleled all-around star (he played and excelled at virtually every position) and future Hall of Famer, Cincinnati native Buck Ewing returned home from his successful years with the Giants in the 1880s to replace Charles Comiskey as Reds manager in the summer of 1895. Over the final five seasons of the century the versatile Ewing became one of the most successful managers in team history, amassing 394 career wins and a lifetime .570 victory pace. Such was the stature of Buck Ewing in his own primitive baseball era that at the time of his premature death caused by Bright's Disease in 1906 the local headlines mourned the passing of one of the game's true giants: "Great catcher dead at his East End home . . . Best all-around player in history."

latest challenge to the reserve clause – the formation of a divisive Players' League – by encouraging American Association owners to expand to a dozen teams for 1890. The move had its calculated results for the National League owners, of course, as the Players' League lasted but one strife-torn season and the financially overextended American Association was of necessity itself absorbed into the National League after the 1891 season.

Rejoining the senior circuit wars in 1890, the Reds went on to amass a decade-long mark of 729-639 (.534). This was certainly short of disastrous, yet it brought only two finishes (1896 and 1898) as high as third place and no single season within 10 games or less of the circuit leader. The best club of the decade was undoubtedly the 1896 team, one which benefitted from the first blockbuster trade in franchise history, a pioneering deal that brought hurler Red Ehret (18-14 that year) and catcher Heinie Peitz (.299 BA) over from St. Louis. Finishing a strong third behind Baltimore (led by the

3. The Birth of National League Tradition in the Queen City

One of the first in a long line of Cuban big league athletes, Dolph Luque joined Cincinnati in 1918 (6-3, 3.80 ERA), and compiled a 170-152 mark the next dozen summers there.

Something extraordinary happened along the downtown banks of the Ohio River in the sleepy city of Cincinnati on the afternoon of April 16, 1990. The venerable baseball club known for nearly a century and a quarter as the Cincinnati Reds opened up the home portion of the first National League baseball season in a new decade before a large but non-sellout throng of 38,000, downing the San Diego Padres 2-1 for the club's fifth consecutive win to start the young campaign. But it was not the winning streak (although the club's fastest start in years, which reached a club-record 10 straight before it was halted) that was the real story. The home opener was being played after a week on the road, an ordinary enough occurrence for about half the league's ballclubs each year. Only in this case it was indeed extraordinary – the end to a nearly century-long tradition in a sport whose very warp and fabric is the gossamer stuff of traditions and airy nostalgia.

Opening Day of the baseball season had, after all, become over the years a full-scale national tradition in the oldest of all National League cities. As one wag has put it, it is the single honor bestowed upon America's first baseball city by the Lords of Baseball, that it should have the consolation of the season's first game, a fitting compensation for being as often found at the bottom of the league standings as on the top of the innovators' list. Another humorist once noted that Cincinnati was the city where everyone flocked to the ballpark on Opening Day and then stayed home throughout the remainder of the summer. But however misguided the humor, it is indeed true that Opening Day has long been Cincinnati's proudest baseball badge.

This time-honored tradition of league home openers dates back to the tireless effort and considerable vision of early team executive Frank C. Bancroft, one-time theatrical agent and Reds business manager from the early National League days of 1891 until his death 30 years later. Relying on his expertise in theatrical promotion and his raw enthusiasm for his newfound baseball passion, Bancroft annually stirred such wintertime enthusiasm for the forthcoming edition of the Reds each new season that he regularly sold out first-game tickets months before the crack of the first bat in April signified the renewal of each season. What began as purely profit-motive ticket promotion soon was established as festive civic occasion, and by the time of Banny's death in 1921 Opening Day had become a phenomenon. Schools were closed for the occasion, offices shut down, electricity filled the air, and citizens marched through the streets in a special celebration of baseball's rites of spring unmatched in any other league city. And so it remained up to the World War II years, when league officials began formally recognizing baseball's oldest city with a ceremonial first league game – and so it has remained down to the present.

The first two decades of the new century brought an all-too-familiar story – season after dull season buried in the middle of the National League pack for the talent-thin Cincinnati team of popular owner Garry Herrmann. Seventeen of these 19 seasons would mark finishes in fourth place or below. Two remarkable pitchers, however, enlivened Cincinnati baseball throughout these otherwise barren years that stretched out before the First World War. The first was Frank "Noodles" Hahn, a slight but ferocious moundsman who won 22 games for three successive seasons in 1901-03, all for teams which badly floundered almost any time Hahn himself was not upon the hill. Noodles Hahn tossed a 1900 no-hitter, then struck out 16 batters for a single-game club record which would stand until bested by Jim Maloney as late as 1965. He had already won 121 league games before turning 26; but before turning 27, Hahn had injured his arm and was tragically out of baseball altogether less than a year later.

The second remarkable pitcher of this era was the hard-throwing Fred Toney, a mammoth 245-pound righthander who won 24 games for the 1917 Reds and established a reputation over his 12-year career as one of the best-hitting pitchers gracing the game. Yet Fred Toney will live on in baseball's collective memory for one single remarkable outing still unique to sporting history. The matchup with the Cubs' Jim "Hippo" Vaughn (another colossal pitching heavyweight) was played in old Weeghman Park – forerunner to Chicago's venerable Wrigley Field – on January 11, 1917, and was indeed one of the two or three most memorable and bizarre games in all of baseball's long and unpredictable history. Perhaps only the losing 12-inning perfect-game effort of Harvey Haddix in 1957, or the remarkable 4-0 no-hitter loss of Andy Hawkins in 1990, can match it for exceptional occurrence. For on that day, for the only time in big-league history, two pitchers conspired to throw a double no-hitter against each other for a full nine innings. And in a final fitting irony of the kind with which baseball is so replete, the batter who eventually delivered the game-deciding blow was one of the nation's most storied athletes from a bygone era, one whose role in this game and in baseball as a whole lies almost entirely forgotten to history: Olympic hero and full-blooded

Fred Toney will be remembered in baseball history as a winner of the only double no-hit game ever, a victory over Cubs' ace Hippo Vaughn on May 2, 1917. That same season the iron-armed Toney also hurled 340 innings, recorded a mark of 24-16, and won both ends of a July 1st doubleheader against the Pirates.

BROWN vs. MATHEWSON
GREATEST TREAT OF THE YEAR for BASEBALL FANS

CINCINNATI, OHIO, SEPT. 1, 1916.

"YOU CAN POSITIVELY COUNT ON MY PITCHING AGAINST BROWN ON SEPT. 4th."

CHRISTY MATHEWSON,

MANAGER CINCINNATI REDS.

CHRISTY MATHEWSON

BROWN'S TWIRLING HAND

"THREE FINGERED" BROWN

CHICAGO, ILL.
"MORDECAI BROWN WILL BE READY TO BATTLE AGAINST MATHEWSON LABOR DAY."

JOE TINKER,
MANAGER CUBS.

—1916—

| First Game at 1:30 P.M. | **DOUBLE HEADER LABOR DAY** | First Game at 1:30 P.M |

WEEGHMAN PARK

STARS OF MANY YEARS TO PITCH FOR CHICAGO CUBS AND CINCINNATI REDS

NORTH CLARK AND ADDISON STREETS.
RESERVED SEATS AT A. G. SPALDING & BROS., 28 S WABASH AVE. TEL. CEN. 448.

THE DAILY NEWS BOYS BAND WILL RENDER MUSIC

The immortal Christy Mathewson hurled 635 games for McGraw's New York Giants and but one for the Reds of Cincinnati. The single contest, and the last of the great Matty's career, was a much-ballyhooed start against his long-time rival Three Finger Brown, also appearing in his very last big league contest. The game was played in Chicago (at Weeghman Park, an earlier name for Wrigley Field) and Matty came home with the victory to edge out Brown 13-12 over their heated career rivalry.

Indian Jim Thorpe, a reserve Reds out-fielder for only part of that single season, stroked the second hit of the Reds' tenth-inning uprising, a slow roller along the third baseline which sent home shortstop Larry Kopf with the game's only and deciding run.

Considerable changes in the now tedious baseball fortunes experienced yearly by the River City of Cincinnati soon coincided rather fortuitously with the long-coveted arrival of an established big-league hero, in this case the incomparable Christy Mathewson of the New York Giants. Mathewson ironically had been lost to Cincinnati at the very outset of the Hall of Fame career which would instead bring him 373 big-league victories while laboring for McGraw in the Polo Grounds. Owning the original draft rights to Matty, Cincinnati peddled him to the Giants in the club's worst trade ever, receiving in exchange a sore-armed Amos Rusie who had not been able to pitch for over a year. (It seems that Reds' outgoing owner John T. Brush was about to close a deal to purchase the Giants and was looking to stock his new team with enough talent to assure victory when he himself got there.) Yet if Mathewson

figured in possibly the worst trade of franchise history, he also stood prominently in the middle of one of the very best as well. Sixteen seasons and 372 victories after his unfortunate departure from the Cincinnati fold, Matty was now brought back in July 1916 as part of the only deal ever to land a ballclub three future Hall of Famers in the course of a single transaction (Edd Roush and Bill McKechnie were the other principles). Mathewson had been brought to Cincinnati to take over as manager, and he would make only one final mound appearance in Reds colors, a staged affair against his old rival Three Finger Brown at Weeghman Park in September 1916.

By 1918 the team of Roush and company that third-year manager Mathewson had put together over a few short summers began to show some measurable improvement, edging its way above .500 (68-60) and solidifying a third-place finish. Roush batted .333 and teammate Heinie Groh hit .320, good enough for second and third among league batsmen, behind Brooklyn's own hitting machine Zack Wheat. With Roush (the 1919 league-leader at .321) and Groh (.310) continuing to pound the league's pitchers in 1919, and with Hod

Eller (20-9), Slim Sallee (21-7) and Dutch Ruether (19-6) now forming the best starting trio around, rookie manager Pat Moran was able to lead his charges home nine full games ahead of the runner-up John McGraw team. Mathewson would be gone amidst controversy and personal disillusionment before the end of his third Cincinnati season. Yet the proud Matty deserves a lion's share of the credit for the triumphs that lay hidden around the next bend.

The National League campaign of 1919 was indeed a remarkable one for the perennial doormat ballclub that had regularly resided in the Queen City of Cincinnati since the earliest days of league play. The season's winning percentage of .686 (96-44) would permanently stand as the best in franchise history, even after the Big Red Machine years of the 1970s. While considered no match in the upcoming World Series for a Chicago White Sox team considered one of the best in all baseball history, the Reds had actually won nine

more regular season games than had the Chicago ballclub. And perhaps most noteworthy of all, the final missing cogs in this first pennant-winning Cincinnati machine of the modern era had been only hastily inserted the previous off-season when likeable owner Garry Herrmann had swung deals for first baseman Jake Daubert, second sacker Morrie Rath, and shortstop Larry Kopf, building an entire new infield around talented third sacker Heinie Groh. And if this were not enough, the astute Herrmann had earlier rescued seemingly washed up hurler Slim Sallee – about to enjoy his proverbial career season – plucking the grateful lefty off the waiver list from none other than his closest pennant contenders, John McGraw's New York Giants.

The World Series of 1919 has received more press than all but a handful of dramatic and fateful Series clashes – the Giants and Indians in 1954, the Yankees and Dodgers the following autumn, the Cardinals and Tigers in 1968 or the Reds

Below left: Horace "Hod" Eller enjoyed a short yet productive five-year big league career with the Reds in which he posted a 61-40 mark and 2.62 ERA. Eller peaked in the 1919 pennant year with 20 victories, a World Series shutout in Game 5, and title-clinching complete-game victory in the Black Sox Series finale.

Below: Pat Moran was a rookie manager the season the Reds won their first World Title ever in 1919.

Above: *Cincinnati's first World Champion team poses for a photo during the 1919 NL season. Only the clubs of 1939-40 and 1962 won more games in a season before the Big Red Machine era than did the 1919 Champions, owners of 96 wins.*

Opposite top: *Joe Jackson of Chicago is cut down at second base in a failed steal attempt during 1919 Series Game One. Larry Kopf, who once broke up the Toney-Vaughn double no-hit game, is the Cincy shortstop making the tag on Shoeless Joe.*

Opposite bottom: *Series action in a fully decked-out Redland Field during Game One of the now infamous Black Sox World Series.*

and Red Sox in 1975. What is seemingly forgotten in all the hoopla surrounding eight infamous Chicago turncoats, however, is the fine Series play of a talented and inspired Cincinnati nine. The bare facts of that Series have now been rehearsed in novels, films and even serious scholarly tomes. While the underdog Reds managed to pull an upset of major proportions by besting the powerhouse White Sox team of tight-pocketed Chicago owner Charles Comiskey five games to three, the baseball world had smelled a rotting fishpile from early on in Series play. A year later it would be determined by newly installed commissioner Judge Kenesaw Mountain Landis that eight Sox stars had conspired with gamblers to throw the Series; the revelation, which shook the baseball world to its very foundations, would mean a lifetime ban from the sport for all eight, including certain Hall of Famer Joe Jackson. No matter that a Chicago grand jury had already acquitted the banished eight of all such charges. The less-bare fact of World Series 1919 is that the undaunted and unintimidated Reds had bolted from the gate to a 4-1 Series lead behind the brilliant pitching of Eller, Ruether, Sallee and Jimmy Ring (a previously unheralded spot pitcher with a Series 0.64 ERA over 14 innings). Taking full advantage of a nine-game Series format utilized briefly in 1919-21, the Cincinnati club then held on doggedly to win on

Hod Eller's second complete-game victory in game eight.

Another long-overshadowed feature of the 1919 World Series was the historic role of skilled Cincinnati relief pitcher Adolfo Luque, a fair-skinned foreigner from the Caribbean island-nation of Cuba, and first of his countrymen to taste the thrill of World Series play. One of a small handful of non-black Cubans who was able to boast big league experience in the early decades of the century, Luque had first stuck as a spot starter with the Reds at the end of the First World War, appearing in a dozen games in 1918, then shifting to relief chores in 1919 and posting a 9-3 season's mark, winning three games in relief and saving three more. In the ill-starred 1919 Series Luque would relieve brilliantly for five innings spread over two games, allowing but one hit and striking out eight. By the following season he was an established starter, posting a 13-9 record, and for the next nine summers Luque would regularly post double-digit victory seasons on the hill for the Reds. In a baseball epoch now so full of Latin American talent, and after the Hall of Fame careers of the likes of Juan Marichal, Roberto Clemente and Luis Aparicio, it has been lost in the cracks of history that the Reds' pioneering Adolfo Luque was indeed the first of his Spanish-speaking countrymen to set foot in baseball's World Series play.

4. Cincinnati's Game in the Golden Big-Stick Era

One of the game's immortal pitchers, Christy Mathewson's managerial career reached no such glories during his three seasons in Cincinnati. Assuming the reigns of a seventh-place outfit midway into the 1916 campaign, Matty was around for but two more seasons, both fourth-place finishes.

The greatest ironies surrounding the tainted Fall Classic of 1919 were yet to unfold, of course. While the Reds were winners on the field of battle in October 1919, a certain long-standing pall – almost a curse – was soon to fall over both once-proud franchises which had given Americans a World Series so damaging to the nation's faith in its sporting pastimes. As though it were somehow their just dessert as accidental co-conspirators, the innocent and victorious Reds would not again taste pennant fever for two full decades; the sinful Chicago Pale Hose would not again know the joy of hoisting a championship flag for exactly 40 summers. The Pale Hose, then, seem to have had the clear edge on futility, if one tallies up only the number of pennants won as a measure of baseball penance. Yet, as the next three decades unfolded, it is indeed hard to say which club had been seemingly more cursed. In the 19 full seasons before

their next pennant triumph, the Cincinnatians and their stoic fans would experience 13 second-division finishes, 11 of them in a row falling after 1927. The White Sox would count 16 such seasons over the same stretch. The Reds would, in actuality, play at over a .500 clip for most of the 1920s (a last "deadball decade" when pitching was still in vogue) and not plumb the depths of despair until the 1930s rolled in (the era of the modern slugger when "big bats" took over the national game). But misfortune enough indeed lay immediately around the corner for the proud Cincinnati ballclub which seemed to be coming off such a remarkable World Series high as the Roaring Twenties first burst forth upon an optimistic and prosperous post-war nation.

One of the true tragedies of the Reds story in those seasons immediately surrounding 1919 is the saga of the final years of the immortal Christy Mathewson. Matty was the greatest pitcher of an age replete with pitching greats. Featuring a "magic pitch" that was the precursor to today's screwball, Mathewson today still ranks behind only Cy Young and Walter Johnson in career victories, yet more remarkably, perhaps, breezed through most games throwing only 75 or 80 pitches, and walked only 1.6 batters for nine innings throughout his 17-year career. As important to his legend were his striking good looks and college education, which in an age of sports ruffians made Matty the first national baseball idol. Mathewson was never destined for success in the Queen City, however, and only a few short seasons after his arrival he was to depart in a cloud of intrigue and bitter personal disappointment. The true culprit here seemed to be the heavy-hitting yet highly unsavory character that held down the first baseman's post in Cincinnati for three seasons after 1916, one Hal Chase. While Chase's first season with the Reds was the most productive of his career and featured a league batting title (.339 in 1916), questions constantly surrounded the integrity of his play and rumors linked him to efforts by gamblers to fix games. So strong were these charges that Mathewson

in his new capacity as manager suspended Chase for the balance of the season in August 1918. When Chase filed a civil suit against his manager and subsequently was tried by the league itself, he was found innocent of any charge or implication of impropriety (an acquittal which had more to do with League President Heydler's unwillingness to admit dishonesty within the game than with Chase's own freedom from guilt). Matty, for his own part, was disheartened enough by the affair to retire 10 games from season's end and to enlist promptly for military service, which would tragically bring a training exercise accident involving poison gas which led directly to tuberculosis and premature death at age 47. Mathewson's final year in Reds flannels was clearly not one which shed kind light upon the contemporary world of baseball. Nor were the off-field events of his final season in Cincinnati ones which showed the Queen City baseball franchise to its best advantage either. If the Reds were beneficiaries of crooked play in the World Series of 1919, they had experienced their own sordid brush with gambling elements in the game little more than a season earlier.

But if the trade which brought Christy Mathewson to Cincinnati was one which set in motion the wheels of personal pain and disillusionment for the fabled Matty, this had also been a trade which would open one of the brightest chapters in the story of Cincinnati baseball. Another important addition to the growing Cincinnati arsenal in that memorable July 1916 deal with the Giants was the stellar outfielder Edd Roush, perhaps the best all-around fly-chaser in Cincinnati big-league history. Few if any would debate that Roush was the best Cincinnati hitter before Rose. Like Rose, he was a singles-hitter who became one of the best paid players of his era. Roush was to be the first legitimate franchise Hall of Famer years down the road, when the Hall of Fame would become an institution as noble and nostalgia-driven as the Reds baseball club itself. Yet a decade before baseball's permanent memorial in Cooperstown was conceived, Edd Roush was reeling off 10 straight seasons in which he never batted lower than .321, batted five times above .340 and copped two National League batting crowns (1917, 1919) in the process.

Of course there had been some great hitters in Cincinnati before Edd Roush. Wahoo Sam Crawford (a Hall of Famer, after his brilliant 15-year residence with Detroit) stayed only briefly (1899-1902), yet left a considerable mark by leading the league in home runs one season (16 in 1901) and triples (23) the next. Cy Seymour en-

Left: *Only Pete Rose can rival Edd Roush as the greatest hitter in Reds history, and then it must be noted that the latter boasts a lifetime average 20 points higher than the former. Roush was unchallenged as the most feared National League batsman of the dead-ball era, hitting .300 or more for 11 straight seasons. He also employed the heaviest bats in the circuit, weighing between 46 and 68 ounces, and once slapped out seven hits in a single season on pitchouts.*

Left: *Hal Chase was one of the most paradoxical ballpark figures in the history of the dead-ball epoch. A slick-fielding first sacker, he was rated by many of his era as the best gloveman in the league. Only a .291 lifetime hitter, he won a batting title with the Reds in 1916. He also threw games for easy money and was eventually suspended from baseball for life.*

Left: *World Champion Reds manager Pat Moran (left) poses with two of the game's leading figures, colorful Brooklyn field boss Wilbert "Uncle Robbie" Robinson (center) and Dodgers' club owner Charles Ebbets. Moran managed four more seasons in Cincinnati after 1919, finishing second in both 1922 and 1923. Moran died suddenly in March 1924 on the eve of spring training.*

Above: *Forty-nine-year-old veteran minor league skipper Jack Hendricks took over the bench job in Cincinnati when Pat Moran died suddenly on the eve of the 1924 campaign. He remained for six seasons, but only in 1926 did any of his teams challenge for a league title, with a second-place finish.*

Opposite: *Lefty Eppa Rixey achieved two milestones in a 21-year career: He was the NL's winningest southpaw ever before Warren Spahn, and he was also its largest loser. He still ranks seventh among all pitchers in games lost (266-251).*

joyed a burst of Cincinnati stardom even briefer than that of Crawford (1903-05), but hardly less spectacular, as he batted .342, .313 and a remarkable .377, the latter still a club record for single-season excellence. Hal Chase, for all his infamy, had also been a hitter of considerable renown and a second league batting champion for the Reds during the era, when his heady 1916 campaign also produced a league-best in hits with 184. But any such list of accomplished batsmen of early franchise history must also include the famed Heinie Groh, acquired from the cooperative Giants in a 1913 deal involving five players and cash. Groh is best known today for his unusual "bottle bat" with its thin handle and non-tapered barrel. Groh was an outstanding leadoff man whose peculiar wide-open stance and deft batting eye enhanced his offensive specialties – drawing the base-on-balls and dropping down the deadly successful bunt. Though his best years were to come after he returned to the Giants in 1922, for eight seasons Groh was one of the finest hitters ever to perform on Redland Field.

With Roush and Groh and a supporting cast slugging the ball throughout the 1920s, there was firepower aplenty to entertain the fans, but hardly enough for a significant move up in the league's standings. Only the 1923 team – riding the surprising pitching arm of Dolph Luque – and the 1926 squad – with another fine one-year mound wonder in Pete Donohue – challenged seriously for league titles. Luque would enjoy the finest single season of his career in 1923, and arguably the best single campaign ever contributed by a Cincinnati moundsman. Twenty-seven victories (enhanced by a league-best 1.93 ERA) not only paced all senior circuit hurlers that sum-

mer, but also established a Cincinnati team standard equalled only by Bucky Walters' superlative effort 16 summers down the road. Righty Donohue also enjoyed a career plateau three seasons later by pasting together 20-win efforts in both 1925 and 1926. A third sensational moundsman, Eppa Rixey, also pitched brilliantly at times during the first decade after the Great War, with a league-best 25-13 mark in 1922 and two additional 20-win performances over the next three summers, yet Rixey's best years unfortunately corresponded with remarkably uninspired team play. The lackluster Reds ballclubs for which he hurled for 13 summers played a not-insignificant roll in making Eppa Rixey a pitcher of remarkable contrast – the winningest left-hander in baseball history (266) before Warren Spahn appeared on the scene, yet also seventh-biggest loser (251) ever to stride upon a major league rubber. And there were plenty of individual hitting honors to go around throughout the decade, as well. Bubbles Hargrave won a single batting title (.353 in 1926) and thus became the first catcher ever to turn such a feat. Roush won two titles in his first three Cincinnati summers, while Jake Daubert brought his considerable defensive skills at first base over from Brooklyn in time for the 1919 championship run and then carried some heavy lumber for the Redlegs of manager Pat Moran as well.

The worst Reds team of the Roaring Twenties was the 1929 version, an occurrence which did not of course bode well for the new decade on the horizon. Age had overtaken the ballclub which Jack Hendricks inherited from Moran after 1923, and the departure of Roush to the Giants in 1927 signalled the final stages of a doleful decline. When bats boomed around the rest

Above: *Reds' stellar catcher between 1932 and 1941, Ernie "Schnozz" Lombardi, had big hands, a big heart, and a big nose. He also swung a very big bat, hitting over .300 seven times in his decade at Cincy, and along the way became the only receiver ever to win two batting titles. Lombardi was also noted for his slow running, which made his lofty averages all the more impressive.*

Right: *Ace Paul Derringer here demonstrates his famed high-kick delivery which made him one of the NL's most feared moundsmen during the Reds' 1939-40 pennant years.*

of the league during the incredible hitting year of 1930, those in Cincinnati were now strangely silent. The entire National League hit at an astounding .303 pace that unforgettable year, yet Cincinnati came in with a league-worst .281, an altogether unexpected turn for a team whose bats had been so potent across the deadball era only a few seasons earlier.

Things would pick up later in the decade, but only after a string of four last-place finishes which made the seasons of 1931-34 a low-water mark for Cincinnati rooters everywhere. Plucked off the Brooklyn roster in 1932 (along with Babe Herman, in exchange for second baseman Tony Cuccinello and receiver Clyde Sukeforth), strapping Ernie Lombardi slowly improved as the decade wore on, and by 1935 the much-loved "Schnozz" was to begin a string of four remarkable hitting years which saw his batting average range between .333 and .343, placing him among the league's best. Lombardi was famed around the circuit for his lack of speed and his relentless bat, yet he was far more than a one-dimensional hitter. He was one of the league's most durable and dependable receivers and would soon catch Johnny Vander Meer's two remarkable no-hitters at decade's end. Hitting was his forte, however, and with infielders playing him so deep as to leave almost no outfield grass exposed, Lombardi was forced to rely solely on powerful line smashes which streamed from his oversized 44-ounce bat. But above all else Lombardi was a remarkable baseball rarity, a catcher who could hit well enough to win not one but two batting titles, an accomplishment not boasted by any other man in baseball's long history.

The pitching was also improving under short-term managers Dan Howley (1930-32) and Donie Bush (1933), thanks in large part to the arrival of franchise-builder Paul Derringer. Derringer, who today ranks third on the club's all-time winning list, had already helped the Cardinals to a 1931 league flag with a rookie 18-8 mark (garnering the league's best winning percentage) before coming to Cincinnati in a surprise 1933 trade for popular shortstop Leo Durocher. While Derringer's first summer in a Cincinnati uniform was less than spectacular (7-27, 3.30 ERA), he was a remarkable pressure pitcher whose best years would come as the Reds moved into pennant races late in the decade. Paul Derringer would start and win the first major league night game in Cincinnati in 1935, string together three consecutive 20-win seasons in 1938-40, and enjoy a remarkable 25-7 1939 campaign to lead Cincinnati out of its long pennant drought.

Toney) that would achieve instant baseball immortality. It was a stellar yet not particularly remarkable moment when the erratic fastballing lefty no-hit the Boston Bees on June 11, 1938, in Cincinnati's Crosley Field. Four days later, however – in a ballgame that should have drawn its significance from its stature as the first Ebbets

Far left: *Johnny Vander Meer displays the leg action with which he dazzled Braves and Dodgers batsmen during his unprecedented and never-duplicated back-to-back no-hitters on June 11th and June 15th of 1938. Vander Meer posted a lifetime losing record (119-121), yet he did post several solid big league seasons, including an 18-12 mark in 1942 and 17-14 in 1948, also leading the NL in strikeouts three times (1941-43).*

Left: *Reds owner Powel Crosley (left) chats about strategy with his manager Bill McKechnie before the start of the third game of the 1939 World Series. A manufacturing magnate and industrial innovator, Crosley produced the first American small-sized car (which bore his name), built early refrigerators under the label "Shelvador," and founded one of the most powerful radio stations in the land (today still known as WLW). In 1934 Crosley was happily convinced by Larry MacPhail to purchase the failing Cincinnati ballclub. From that point on, he owned and operated the Reds for 27 years, and he was still club president at the time of his death in 1961.*

Another remarkable pitching legend was the remarkable "Dutch Master" Johnny Vander Meer, baseball's all-time exemplar of the single brief moment of diamond glories. Vander Meer's considerable legend was somewhat like that of Fred Toney's two decades earlier, resting on one spectacular achievement and not on the years of consistent toil which earned recognition for stable hurlers like Rixey and Derringer. For Vander Meer it was two incredible games and not one (as was the case with Field night game – Vander Meer proved unhittable once again, setting down the Dodgers 6-0 with the aid of dim arch-lights and untouchable "heat" from his flaming delivery. Never before or since (though another remarkable Cincinnati hurler would later come tantalizingly close) had a big-league pitcher authored two no-hitters in consecutive trips to the mound. A lifetime loser (119-121) who often struggled with control of his lively fastball, Vander Meer had nonetheless made himself a last-

Above: *Reds hurler Junior Thompson greets rival hurler Lefty Gomez of the Yankees before Game 3 of the 1939 World Series. Thompson was the loser that day, 7-3, but Gomez was not around himself long enough to earn the pitching victory.*

Opposite: *The scene is the joyous Reds' dressing room right after the Cincinnati ballclub had clinched its first league title in two full decades by defeating St. Louis 5-3. The date is September 29, 1939, and winning Cincy pitcher Paul Derringer is at the center of this crowd of celebrating mates.*

ing baseball legend with but two unmatched outings in the mid-summer of his second big-league season.

The pitching improvement that had been built around Derringer and Vander Meer was solidified in another great Reds trade when Bucky Walters was acquired from the Phillies in a seemingly inconsequential deal in June 1938. Converted from third base to the mound by the Phillies in 1934, Walters led the league in victories his first two seasons in Redsland (27-11 in 1939 and 22-10 in 1940), and the results of this new tandem of Derringer and Walters surpassed anything seen in Crosley Field since Eller and Sallee. With new manager Bill McKechnie now at the helm, the Reds jumped into the 1939 pennant race as a surprise entry. The acquisition of third sacker Bill Werber (from the Athletics for cash in March 1939) had provided a missing link in an otherwise now solid ballclub, and the Reds surged through early and mid-season, inching ahead of the favored Cardinals and the strong Dodgers now piloted by ex-Reds shortstop Leo Durocher. In late September Derringer clinched the long-awaited pennant with a hard-fought 5-3 victory over the challenging Cardinals in the finale of a

crucial three-game series at Crosley Field.

The World Series of 1939 would prove something of an embarrassment – four straight losses to the powerful New York Yankees, a team batting average of only .203 (Lombardi hit but .214) and only an opening game that was at all close. The Yankees were an awesome outfit featuring an outfield of DiMaggio, Keller and Selkirk and a middle infield of Frankie Crosetti and Joe Gordon, and the Reds were outclassed from the first. But a corner had been turned. The pieces now seemed in place for several years of success. Of course, it should perhaps not be forgotten that the last time the Reds had won a pennant, disaster in the form of a World Series fix would strike the national game. In the post-pennant euphoria of winter 1939, events were again transpiring – this time far beyond baseball's grandstands and fences – which would soon throw the national pastime into a tailspin which would again threaten its very existence. Given the global and diamond events which followed the Reds' only two pennant triumphs of 1919 and 1939, the cynic might secretly speculate that it was indeed a good thing the Cincinnatians did not win more league flags than they did!

5. Innovative Wartime Baseball in Crosley Field

No single decade of baseball play – at least none since the shaping of the modern game during the 1880s – so changed the face of our national sport as did the war-ridden decade of the 1940s. The five years of global fighting which broke out across Europe and in the Pacific theater would reach eventually into every phase of American life, as has no national war effort in this country before or since. And baseball was shaken to its very roots as a result. While some might argue that only four brief inconsequential seasons – 1942-45 – experienced such major inconveniences as dismantled rosters, disappearing box office throngs, slapstick play, restricted travel, and shortened schedules, none can dispute that individual player careers were frequently disrupted, occasionally unpredictably launched, and sometimes tragically halted. Players joined the war effort in droves while wet-eared youngsters (such as the Reds' 15-year-old pitcher Joe Nuxhall)

and the disabled (such as the Browns' one-armed outfielder Pete Gray) stayed home to man the major league infields and outfields. Spring training was radically altered as well by wartime travel restrictions, with disgruntled ballplayers working out their inevitable winter kinks in such frigid venues as West Lafayette, Indiana and Medford, Massachusetts. Benefitting from a league-wide neutralization of talent that had descended like a pall by 1944, the stumblebum St. Louis Browns would make their only post-season appearance in a laugh-filled half-century of American League existence. The fans' baseball passions turned elsewhere as the war effort heated up and patriotic causes supplanted pennant races. And yet through it all the national treasure of baseball became a vital wartime emotional prop, its very daily appearance in the ballparks and on the sports pages seemingly crucial to morale back home and the national war effort on the distant

A one-armed outfielder, lame-armed pitchers, and "wet-behind-the-ears" youngsters – all appeared in the big leagues in the war-torn years of the early 1940s. Fifteen-year-old Hamilton High School star Joe Nuxhall appeared on the hill for the Reds for the first time on June 10, 1944. Here preparing with skipper McKechnie for his debut, Nuxhall hurled less than a full inning, yet was the youngest player ever to appear on a major league diamond.

battlefield. What, after all, were American boys fighting and dying for, if not for baseball and a taste of mom's apple pie?

Radical change storming across the face of baseball had, of course, already made an appearance long before the rude jolt of Pearl Harbor. And a focal point for that change was once more the innovative baseball franchise belonging to Cincinnati. But whereas so many other innovations fostered by Cincinnati baseball down through the years – the seventh-inning stretch, the catcher's squat, a league-first switch hitter or unprecedented double play – had "just sort of happened casually" as a byproduct more of circumstance than forethought, what came to National League baseball via the Queen City in the immediate pre-war years were the carefully orchestrated strategies of one of baseball's greatest entrepreneurial innovators. The motivating force behind this latest change which soon swept across the national pastime was the noisy tinkerer and flamboyant hothead Larry MacPhail, an innovative genius usually not talked about today in the same breath with Bill Veeck or Charlie Finley or Branch Rickey. Yet MacPhail was every bit as much a revolutionary giant as Veeck or Finley in his lasting influences upon the game. First there came radio baseball in Cincinnati in the mid-1930s with the debut of honey-throated southerner Red Barber (who would eventually follow MacPhail to

Brooklyn in 1938). Then there was the experiment of night baseball in 1935, with the Reds and Paul Derringer defeating Philadelphia 2-1 before more than 20,000 curious patrons on May 24 in major league baseball's first arch-light game. Soon there was a team travelling by air, as MacPhail chartered two American Airlines planes to motor his charges to Chicago in 1934, then flew the team from the Dominican Republic to Miami after a springtime exhibition two seasons later. The progressive management of MacPhail would introduce the season ticket plan and the flashing "E" on the Crosley Field scoreboard to inform fans of scoring decisions during the 1934 season as well. And in the midst of all this tinkering with tradition, Larry MacPhail would also demonstrate his considerable baseball savvy by pasting together a Cincinnati team that would be a solid pennant winner by the time he himself was ensconced in Brooklyn at decade's end.

If the winds of change were blowing strong before this new decade progressed beyond its earliest months, this change seemed but a temporary distraction for the solid ballclub taking the field daily in Cincinnati. For the Reds were now engaged in the surprising business of defending a pennant, a fact which in itself was quite a radical departure from the usual bleak saga of Cincinnati baseball fortunes. Flush from their pennant success of 1939, the 1940 Reds rumbled home with the second best

Above left: *History-in-the-making is here captured as Redlegs shortstop Billy Myers slides home with the first run ever scored in a big-league night game. The date was May 24, 1935, and the setting was Crosley Field. The run held up as the winning tally when Derringer outdueled Joe Bowman of the Phillies by a score of 2-1.*

Above: *Few if any executives have had quite the same impact on the beloved national pastime as did Larry MacPhail. Launching his hectic career in Cincinnati (1934-36), the fiery MacPhail introduced night-time baseball, commercial air travel, and daily regular season broadcasts to the major league baseball scene.*

Above: *After a brilliant hurling career with the Reds throughout the decade of the 1940s, Bucky Walters also enjoyed a brief and largely unspectacular stint as field manager between August 1948 and September 1949.*

Above right: *Frank McCormick was a Reds mainstay at first base between 1934 and 1945, winning league MVP honors in 1940 and topping the NL in RBIs in 1939.*

season in franchise annals (32 percentage points short of the World Champion 1919 outfit). At long last a club representing Cincinnati won 100 games, dispatching the Dodgers by 12 games behind the league's best fielding and the booming bat of first baseman Frank McCormick, the league's MVP and leader in both hits (191) and doubles (44) as well as runnerup in RBIs (127) and total bases (298). The pennant race was over early as McKechnie's men showed a rare talent for winning the close contests, besting the opponent by a single run in 43 of the team's 100 victories. Bucky Walters dominated the league's pitchers with highwater marks in victories (22) and ERA (2.48) and Derringer was again but a shade behind (20-12, 3.06). While McCormick was the hitting and fielding star (topping his position in putouts, double plays and fielding percentage), Lombardi enjoyed

one more fine season as well, hitting .300 for the final time in a Reds uniform. The tragedy of reserve catcher Willard Hershberger – who took his own life mid-season in a Boston hotel – was therefore but a momentary sour note to an otherwise sterling Cincinnati campaign.

The 1940s Reds entered World Series play as a team with a clearcut mission. This time there would be no embarrassment like the hitting (2.03 Series BA) and pitching (4.33 ERA) collapse which witnessed a four-game shellacking at the hands of the powerful Yankees a year earlier. The Series this time around would be as dramatic and exciting as its 1939 counterpart was lopsided and uninteresting. Play would stretch the full seven games to the wire against the Hank Greenberg-led Detroit Tigers, and in the end the heroes wearing red and grey flannels were Bucky Walters and reliable third sacker Billy Werber. Walters authored two complete-game victories, the second a brilliant shutout effort woven in game six with the Reds on the verge of elimination and spiced by Walters' own eighth-inning homer. Werber batted .370 and tied Greenberg with a Series-high 10 base hits. These Reds were indeed one of history's most underrated champions, and when World Series heroics ended with Jimmy Ripple racing across home plate carrying the lead run in the seventh inning of the Crosley Field finale, McKechnie's men had provided the National League with its first World Series winner since the 1934 Gas House Gang Cardinals had struck down these same Detroiters a half-dozen autumns earlier.

The champions which manager Bill McKechnie had painstakingly pulled together and then inspired down the stretch in 1939-40 did not unravel immediately, despite the subsequent outbreak of European war and the widespread raiding of club rosters that affected virtually all teams after 1942. By the zenith of the war effort, however, the Reds were already "the worst of the worst" among war-ravaged ballclubs of the National and American leagues. A third-place finish in 1944 would mark the last first-division effort until 1956. The 1945 team, in turn, was an all-time low: with only McCormick and shortstop Eddie Miller and a much-diminished Bucky Walters on hand among experienced and talented holdovers, the Reds slumped to the worst record of the McKechnie era — 93 losses and a distant seventh-place finish, 37 games behind the champion Cubs. Against this bleak backdrop, one of the few interesting wartime stories in Cincinnati was the 1944 appearance of baseball's youngest-ever pitcher of the twentieth century, future Reds mound star and long-

Reds outfielder Jimmy Ripple, the Series RBI leader, crosses home plate with his third-inning roundtripper in Game 2 of the 1940 Fall Classic against Detroit. The blast provided the game-winning run as the Reds evened the Series, on their way to an eventual seven-game triumph and second franchise World Championship.

A side-armed "buggy-whip" delivery was this 6'6" stringbean hurler's claim to fame, yet Ewell Blackwell was also one of the most feared NL pitchers of the late 1940s, leading the circuit in wins (22-8), complete games (23), and strikeouts (193) for a fifth-place Reds ballclub.

literally exploded onto the Cincinnati baseball scene in the first months after VE Day and VJ Day. Six-foot six-inch beanpole Ewell Blackwell was the most exciting newcomer in a Cincinnati uniform since Ernie Lombardi had debuted with a .303 rookie batting average in the "Big Stick" era of the 1930s. In his remarkable sophomore season of 1947 Blackwell won 16 in a row, the longest league victory skein since Rube Marquard's 1912 string of 19. During this hot stretch the unorthodox sidewinding hurler even more surprisingly nearly duplicated Vander Meer's unheard-of and still unmatched double no-hit feat of 1938; having goose-egged the Braves in a rare night game on June 18, he next came within one sparse inning of dual perfection in his subsequent outing against Brooklyn, only to have Eddie Stanky ruin the bid with a one-out heart-wrenching single. But it was a brilliant season enough for Blackwell – a true career season – in which "The Whip" paced the senior circuit in wins (22-8), complete games (23) and strikeouts (193) for the otherwise lackluster fifth-place Reds.

Ewell Blackwell was the final glorious story of the wartime baseball years in Redsland. Arm miseries took all the snap out of "The Whip" after that one brilliant summer of 1947, and brief comeback seasons in 1950 (17-15, 2.97 ERA) and 1951 (16-15, 3.45 ERA) never reached the dizzying heights of that first dream season, when National League hitters fell like flies before the exploding sidearm delivery of baseball's most famous stringbean hurler. Before and after Blackwell's brief post-war fling, Cincinnati baseball seemed little more than a painful saga of overachieving journeymen and underachieving prospects. Eddie Miller, who manned the center of the infield from 1942 through 1947, was a fine defensive shortstop with occasional power (19 homers and a league-leading 38 doubles in 1947) who some called the finest at his position in a Reds uniform until the flashy Roy McMillan eventually came along. Stonefaced Hank Sauer brought some needed boom to the ballpark with 35 roundtrippers (surpassing Ival Goodman's club mark of 30) before taking his questionable talents over to the even more lackluster Cubs. Grady Hatton was the league's best-fielding third sacker in 1949 and one of its least offensive-minded hotcorner heroes as well. By the last years of the decade the Reds were from top to bottom a distinctly seventh-place club. Only the hapless Chicago Cubs (a mere half-game in arrears of the Crosley Field campers in 1948 and but a single full game in 1949) kept them from being something less, and then only by the slimmest of margins.

time broadcaster Joe Nuxhall. With a depleted wartime roster in hand and his team already hopelessly out of contention, McKechnie sent Nuxhall to the mound on June 10 for a brief ninth-inning stint against the potent league-leading Cardinals. The nervous 15-year-old Nuxhall (signed by the Reds only with permission of his high school principal) allowed five runs on two hits and five walks while retiring but two St. Louis batters. It would take seven long years of minor league toil before Nuxhall would have a second, less pressure-packed chance to pitch for his hometown ballclub in 1952.

In a decade of surprising phenoms, one-year wonders and brief-flashing diamond dreams, Cincinnati would have its own Horatio Alger as well as its overmatched Baby Wags. When established players drifted back slowly from the war, one gangly returning veteran in particular

Left: *Reds' newly appointed skipper Bucky Walters (right) talks strategy with outfielder Hank Sauer, shortly after it was announced that the Reds' pitching ace would replace Johnny Neun on the bench, on August 6, 1948. Bucky Walters thus became one of the diamond's rarest phenomena, a playing manager who was a pitcher.*

Below: *Reds outfielder Ival Goodman slides safely into third base during heated action in Game 4 of the 1940 World Series with Detroit. Pinky Higgins is the Tigers' third sacker who here dives at the sliding Goodman. The play occurred during the first inning of a game eventually won by Cincinnati, 5-2.*

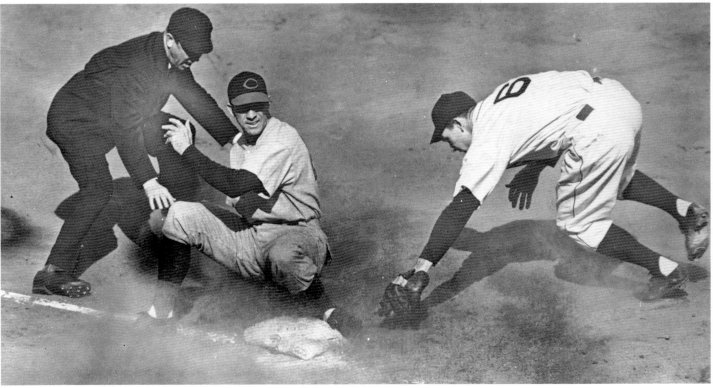

6. Redlegs of Baseball's Fabulous Fifties and Forgotten Sixties

Five imposing baseball figures dominate the epoch of Reds baseball history which stretches from the outbreak of the Korean War through man's first landing upon the surface of the moon. It was an age of unprecedented social and scientific change across the face of the larger nation outside of baseball, as a shrinking world scene transmogrified rapidly from Jet Age into Space Age. Within the nation's ballparks it was an era of staggering change as well, and in America's oldest baseball city these were destined to be the final two memorable decades of exciting diamond action at the venerable old Crosley Field site on Findlay and Western, a setting where baseball had been played without interruption every season since 1884.

Two of these figures – Ted Kluszewski and Frank Robinson – were power-hitting outfielders flush in the mainstream tradition of heavy-hitting Cincinnati ballclubs

of the past. A third – Jim Maloney – was a remarkable but ill-starred pitcher already in danger a mere two decades later of being overlooked by the ebb and flow of unkind baseball fortune. Still another – stoic and genial Fred Hutchinson – remains the most popular manager and perhaps the most tragic figure in Reds history, an immensely popular bench leader who guided the usually humdrum Redlegs to their single sojourn to the top of the National League heap during the three decades which stretch between Pearl Harbor and the close of the Vietnam era. The last though by no means least – young Pete Rose – was still a wet-behind-the-ears favorite son and neophyte baseball legend, first tentatively stretching his wings and testing his muscles in the final lame years before the pennant juggernaut that would soon be known as the Big Red Machine. Cincinnati Reds history of the 1950s and 1960s unavoidably

All-time NL hitting great Rogers Hornsby (wielding the bat) offers some of his batting expertise to his Cincinnati charges during 1953 spring training camp in Tampa. The willing pupils are (l to r) outfielder Wally Post, infielder Rocky Bridges and shortstop Roy McMillan. Hornsby's second and final season as Redlegs manager resulted in a lackluster sixth-place finish.

A sixth baseball relic, old Crosley Field itself, was also to play a prominent role in the story of this chapter of Reds history. Once a haven for pitchers, the compact steel and concrete ballpark had become a paradise for sluggers by the post-World War II years, and in 1948 slow-footed outfielder Hank Sauer rewrote the local record books by clouting 36 roundtrippers for Johnny Neun's seventh-place Reds. But Hank Sauer was quickly enough forgotten in Cincinnati (he was subsequently traded to Chicago in 1949) when muscular left-handed first baseman Ted Kluszewski began smashing the ball with regularity in the early 1950s. Big Klu was an imposing physical specimen who had been signed directly off the Indiana University campus where he had been enrolled as a promising football star, and where the Reds had been forced to hold temporary spring training

headquarters under wartime conditions in the late winter of 1944. Kluszewski started slowly enough in a big league uniform, utilizing his massive frame to launch only 74 homers in his first five full seasons. But by 1952 the strapping young slugger's batting average had soared to .320, and then for four remarkable seasons between 1953 and and 1956 Big Klu went on a relentless tear, smashing 40, 49, 47 and 35 homers and amassing over 100 RBIs in each of those four campaigns.

Buoyed by Kluszewski's personal power outburst, a surge of Reds power hitting was soon launched which would witness 166 team homers in 1953, 147 in 1954, 181 in 1955, and then a league-record 221 circuit blasts in 1956. The 1956 lineup boasted an awesome display of raw muscle from top to bottom of the batting order: first sacker Kluszewski (35 HRs), third baseman Ray Jablonski (15), rightfielder Wally Post (36), centerfielder Gus Bell (29), leftfielder Frank Robinson (38), backstop Ed Bailey (28), and reserves George Crowe (10) and Smokey Burgess (12). This new contingent

It wasn't Murderers' Row, but it certainly was a killer offense. Four of the Reds' greatest sluggers ever here display their lumber in New York, as they set their sights on tying a NL homer mark for two or more roundtrippers in a string of six straight games. The muscular contingent is (l to r) Ted Kluszewski, Gus Bell, Wally Post, and third sacker Ray Jablonski. This awesome 1956 Redlegs lineup went on to smash a record 221 circuit blasts for the full season.

Redlegs' long-ball star Ted Kluszewski here strikes a characteristic "Big Klu" batting pose during 1953 spring training action under a sun-drenched sky in Tampa, Florida. Klu's muscular biceps were both the delight of Redlegs fans and the bane of NL hurlers.

of Crosley Field fence busters was a team the fans could love. So enthralled with their hometown heroes were the Queen City fans, in fact, that at the outset of the following season the Cincinnati faithful would stuff the ballot boxes in the annual league All-Star Game fan voting, an un-precedented development which led to Red-leg starters being selected for all eight field positions with the exception of first base (where Stan Musial and Gil Hodges out-polled Cincy's George Crowe). Commissioner Ford Frick predictably intervened to

remove two fortuitous beneficiaries of such unbridled fan enthusiasm (Roy McMillan and Don Hoak), yet left five Reds (Robin-son, Bell, Post, Bailey, and second sacker Johnny Temple) in the game's starting lineup.

There was certainly plenty to cheer about in Crosley Field besides the explosion of longballs and proliferation of league all-stars as the decade of the fifties entered its second half. The 1956 season saw the power-laden if pitching-short Cincinnati team surge from eleven straight seasons in

either fifth, sixth, or seventh place to a surprising third place finish, a mere two games off the pace set by Brooklyn and a single game behind the resurgent Braves, now relocated in Milwaukee. The charges of third-year skipper Birdie Tebbetts earned over 90 victories for the first time since the pennant seasons of 1939 and 1940, and Cincinnati was not eliminated from the hot pennant race by Brooklyn until the season's final day. It was a banner year for the Reds' faithful and the onslaught of home run excitement, coupled with the rare presence of

a true pennant race, was enough to push Crosley Field attendance well over the million mark for the first time ever. To add sweet icing to the cake, exciting Reds rookie outfielder Frank Robinson tied Wally Berger's 1930 mark for first-year homers and became the first-ever unanimous choice in the league's barely ten-year-old Rookie-of-the-Year balloting.

Kluszewski represented indisputably the most visible and lasting image of the heavy-hitting Reds team of the mid-1950s. The hulking first baseman's bulging biceps

were even responsible for a revolutionary sleeveless uniform design well-suited to a bevy of big-armed sluggers. But Big Klu was more than a lumbering Bunyanesque slugger; he was also a fine all-around hitter who not only led the majors in long balls and RBIs in 1954 but paced the senior circuit as well in total hits the following summer, and batted above .300 in each of his five productive years between 1952 and 1956. Kluszewski was also one of the finest fielding first sackers of his era, pacing his position in fielding a record five straight summers. Injuries drastically cut the big man's effectiveness after 1956, however, and when GM Gabe Paul and field boss Tebbetts decided somewhat unwisely after a fourth-place season in 1957 to exchange slugging for pitching, Klu was unceremoniously dealt off to Pittsburgh before the outset of the 1958 season. The exchange, of course, was not a very good one (despite

Above: *A mid-1950s era of power Redlegs baseball is born as "Birdie" Tebbetts (left) signs on as manager to replace the ousted Rogers Hornsby. The new skipper is here greeted by club owner Powel Crosley (right) and General Manager Gabe Paul (center). The date here is September 29, 1953, and the new boss would remain at the helm of the slugging Redlegs until the middle of the 1958 season. Reds teams under Tebbetts would supply exciting fence-busting action yet would remain in the middle of the pack.*

Right: *Big Klu here crosses home plate with his 14th homer of the 1955 campaign, in which he would blast 47 total round-trippers.*

Left: *Pre-season drills are in full swing for the 1956 Reds outfit in Tampa, Florida. Outfielder Gus Bell here hits the practice sandpit in sliding drills, while manager Birdie Tebbetts watches veteran infielder Roy McMillan make a tag. The upcoming season would be the Redlegs' best under Tebbetts, a tight third-place finish only two games behind the pennant-winning Brooklyn ballclub.*

Kluszewski's obvious declining effectiveness) and the Reds themselves continued to slump, dipping back below .500 in 1958 and tumbling once more into the league's second division the following summer. Skipper Tebbetts himself was gone from the helm before the 1958 campaign was played out, and a brief if glorious era of legendary Redleg power had effectively come to an end after but five short seasons.

Kluszewski's assault on National League fences in the mid-1950s received plenty of hometown support from a contingent of heavy-hitting teammates who supplied a heavy-lumbered lineup even surpassing that fielded by the league's strongboys – the Boys of Summer Dodgers and the Aaron-Mathews-led Milwaukee Braves. Outfielder Wally Post smashed 40 homers of his own in 1955 (with 109 RBIs) and 36 in 1956, yet led the league in strikeouts as well both summers. Smooth-fielding Gus Bell also chipped in 30 homers in 1953 and 27 and 29 during the power years of 1955 and 1956, while enjoying three consecutive 100 RBI years (1953-55) and patrolling center field with great distinction. Catcher Ed Bailey pounded out 28 homers as well during the record-setting roundtripper onslaught of 1956. And George Crowe, Kluszewski's alternate at first base during his final injury-plagued year of 1957, also provided 31 circuit blasts of his own – in a mere 494 at bats.

Yet the heaviest artillery of the homer-crazy season of 1956 belonged to a second imposing figure who fortified Reds baseball in the decade of the fifties – richly talented young outfielder Frank Robinson. Robinson burst onto the National League scene in 1956 with a then-rookie-record 38 homers

(second in the league to Duke Snider), league leadership in runs scored, and a fourth-place league standing in slugging percentage (.558) and total bases (319). A runaway choice as Rookie of the Year in 1956, Robbie would continue to slug homers at an awesome pace in Cincinnati over the entire next decade, amassing 324 in that period, though somehow never once managing to lead the league in this most visible offensive category. Robinson slugged away throughout the remainder of the 1950s and the first half of the 1960s, hitting over .300 on five occasions and winning the league slugging crown three separate times.

A third crucial actor in the Reds' colorful saga of the late 1950s came on board in 1959

Left: *The sudden climb in the league standings by the 1956 power-laden Redlegs was due in large part to the appearance of slugging outfielder Frank Robinson. Shown here early in his rookie campaign, Robbie enjoyed the finest debut season in Cincinnati Reds history, smashing a record-tying 38 homers, leading the senior circuit with 122 runs scored, knocking home 83 more runs, and batting at a .290 clip. It was only the beginning, however, for the 1956 NL Rookie-of-the-Year and future Hall-of-Famer, who would go on to register 586 career homers (fourth best in baseball history), 324 of them in a Reds uniform.*

and would waste little time in converting undying player loyalty into a desperately needed formula for winning baseball. Hutchinson inherited a 1959 team struggling in seventh place which was only able to right itself enough by season's end to rise to a fifth-place tie, despite leading the league in runs scored, batting average and slugging percentage. The still-potent Reds attack was now led by second-year center fielder Vada Pinson, who paced the league in doubles and runs scored while batting .316, as well as by a rapidly maturing Frank Robinson (.311, 36 homers, 125 RBIs) and by veteran second sacker Johnny Temple, sporting a career-high .311 BA. The weakness in this first edition of the Hutchinson-led Reds was clearly in the pitching, where staff leader Bob Purkey (with 13 victories) lost 18 and compiled an unimpressive 4.25 ERA, which was still best among the club starters. Quickly assessing the vital need for front-line pitching, Hutchinson (himself an ex-pitcher) engineered a trade by season's end which brought on board Cleveland hurler Cal McLish, a 19-game winner, in exchange for the veteran Temple. The trade had been a somewhat hasty one, however, as McLish would prove altogether ineffective in the tiny Crosley Field confines and would slump to but four victories in the disastrous sixth-place 1960 season which was to follow.

Hutchinson's second full season in command also offered little of real promise, as the 1960 edition of the Reds fell 20 games below .500 and 28 games off the pennant pace. Robinson and Pinson both slumped below .300 and the team, so recently an offensive powerhouse, couldn't offer a single .300 hitter. The pitching showed some improvement, with the turnaround of 17-game winner Bob Purkey and the surprise showing of young fastballer Jim O'Toole (12-12, 3.80 ERA). Undaunted by his failed first effort to exchange veteran infielders for much-needed pitching, Hutchinson struck again in December of 1960, shipping veteran stellar defensive shortstop Roy McMillan to the Braves for promising bonus-baby hurler Joey Jay, then acquiring a hard-hitting third baseman, Gene Freese, from the White Sox to take over the hot corner while rapidly-improving Eddie Kasko was moved into the vacant shortstop slot. The pieces suddenly seemed to be falling into place for the risk-driven Hutchinson, if only Pinson and Robinson could improve from off seasons in 1960, and youngsters O'Toole and Jay could deliver on their untried pitching promise.

Unsettling change surrounded the Reds in the front office as well as on the diamond when the 1961 season spring training

Above: *"Shake hands and come out fighting" seems to be the catchline for this photo, as managers Fred Hutchinson of Cincinnati and Ralph Houk of the New York Yankees do just that during a workout at Yankee Stadium on October 2, 1961. The two ballclubs were about to open the 1961 World Series two days later.*

Right: *Unsung hero for the 1961 National League champion Reds was outfielder Vada Pinson, the NL's second best hitter that summer with a sterling .343 BA. Over his first five years with the Reds, Pinson averaged 197 hits, 108 runs scored, 37 doubles, 20 home runs, 88 RBIs, 26 stolen bases, and a .310 batting average.*

when Fred Hutchinson inherited the manager's post from interim skipper Mayo Smith, a full 80 games into the 1959 campaign. A talented pitcher with the Tigers in the late 1940s (95-71, 3.73 ERA), Hutch had already enjoyed short managerial stints with the Tigers and Cardinals before being hired on by new Cincinnati GM Frank "Trader" Lane. The new bench boss quickly proved extremely popular with his players camps opened. General Manager Gabe Paul had left to oversee a planned expansion franchise in Houston after the 1960 season. Long-time owner Powel Crosley died suddenly before the ballclub even broke spring training camp. Bill DeWitt was now on board as new GM, faced immediately with sagging attendance brought on by several seasons of mediocre Crosley Field play. When season's play began there was little if anything to foreshadow the upsurge that was just around the corner, as the ballclub won but six of its first twenty-four games. A late April deal which sent veteran catcher Ed Bailey to the Giants for infielder Don Blasingame seemed insignificant enough at the time. The pieces had all fallen silently into place, however, and the revamped Reds closed on the Dodgers and Giants as mid-season progressed. Robinson (.323) and Pinson (.343) again slugged with authority, the latter barely missing out to Pittsburgh's Bob Clemente for the hotly contested league batting crown. Jay sparkled with a league-best 21 victories and O'Toole added 19, while Purkey chipped in 16 and Jim Brosnan added 10 more from the bullpen. The Dodgers lost ten straight in mid-August and the Reds soon slipped in front to stay. By the season's final day Cincinnati held a four-game margin over Los Angeles and the city unleashed its first wild pennant celebration in 21 full seasons. Frank Robinson was league MVP and the gate had predictably doubled over the 1960 season to 1.1 million paying fans. An unexpected World Series slump by Cincinnati bats which would bring a quick five-game victory to a powerful New York Yankees team paced by the slugging duo of Mantle and Maris was only a small tarnish on what had been a delightful surprise season for the long-suffering Cincinnati baseball faithful.

Hutchinson's teams of the next three campaigns could never match their sterling 1961 play, and even an improvement to 98 victories in 1962 could not prevent a fall to third slot behind the runaway Giants and Dodgers. The 1963 ballclub showed improved pitching, as youngster Jim Maloney won 23 (with six shutouts and a 2.77 ERA) and O'Toole contributed 17; but Purkey and Jay were plagued with persistent arm troubles and won but 13 ballgames between them. It was the hitting which broke down altogether, however, as only Pinson remained above .300 (.313 with 22 homers), Robinson slumped to a career-worst .259 (hitting one less homer than Pinson), and the team as a whole logged a .246 mark, only sixth-best in the entire league. The result was a fifth-place finish, still 10 games above .500, yet 13 games off the league-

Left: *A major contribution to the surprise Cincinnati pennant of 1961 was made by Jim O'Toole, the southpaw ace of the NL champion Reds. Enjoying his finest campaign, O'Toole posted a 19-9 won-lost mark and a 3.10 ERA, and also paced Cincinnati starters in game appearances with 39. The battling lefty would win in double figures three more times for the Reds and post a 98-84 standard over his ten-year National League career.*

Left: *Ace of the 1961 champion Redlegs was hard-throwing righty Joey Jay, the very first graduate of Little League baseball to make a major league appearance. Jay posted a league-leading 21-10 mark in 1961, also tying Warren Spahn for the shutout lead with four. Jay would match his 21-victory season in 1962, but never again after that would he enjoy the heights of stardom, winning in double figures only once more with a mediocre 11-11 ledger in 1964.*

Above: *Game action in 1960 at Dodger Stadium features Los Angeles batter Charlie Neal lining out to Reds pitcher Bob Purkey. The Reds receiver here is Dutch Dotterer.*

Right: *Bob Purkey was a standby of the Red mound corps in the late 1950s and early 1960s, posting a 17-11 mark in the 1961 pennant season and pacing the NL in winning percentage (23-5) in 1962.*

leading pace of high-riding Los Angeles.

A dual bright spot in this lackluster 1963 campaign, however, was the simultaneous emergence of two final supernovas in these swansong Crosley Field years of the Reds baseball saga. Jim Maloney had emerged from virtually nowhere as a new and much-needed strong-armed pitching hope. And a brash home-grown rookie second baseman named Pete Rose – logging more plate appearances than anyone wearing the Reds' colors that summer, save tireless veteran Vada Pinson – hit a respectable .273 and, with 170 base knocks, moved to within a mere 4021 career hits of immortal Ty Cobb on the first leg of his three-decade chase after the all-time major league hits leader.

Quite by contrast, the 1964 baseball season in Cincinnati was perhaps the saddest in club history, certainly the one most tinged with human suffering and fraught with raw human emotion. Now almost forgotten in the hindsight of history is the painful fact that the Reds lost yet another pennant that year, this time by dropping four of the final five games after a stirring late drive which saw 11 victories in 12 games and which had put them in first place as late as September 27th. Better remembered than the final week's slump is the sad fact that popular manager Fred Hutchinson – beloved by fans and players alike – had been diagnosed the previous winter as suffering from terminal cancer. Hutch managed bravely throughout the early season, until entering the hospital for treatment in late July. The wan and emaciated skipper returned for several brief stints in August but was finally forced to hand over daily club operations to his assistant Dick Sisler for the fateful September pennant stretch drive. The ballclub gamely battled in an all-out effort to win the flag for

Left: *Slugger Frank Robinson would stroke 37 homers and knock home 124 runs to pace the Redlegs' pennant effort in 1961, then return with 39 roundtrippers and a league-best 134 runs scored during the follow-up third-place campaign. Robbie also led the senior circuit in slugging percentage for three consecutive seasons between 1960 and 1962 and would never hit less than 21 homers in any of his ten Cincinnati campaigns.*

Left: *The back-to-back glory seasons of 1961 and 1962 seemed to lack for an encore as the Redlegs tumbled to fifth slot and only ten games above .500 in 1963. That season was not without its huge plus, however, for in the Cincinnati lineup that disappointing summer was a hustling switch-hitting local boy named Pete Rose, who took over the second-base job from Don Blasingame. Soon Rose was on his way to immortality as baseball's all-time base hits leader and the Queen City's all-time baseball hero.*

their popular skipper, but a Cinderella ending was simply not to be. The pennant was lost in the waning weeks as a wild finish saw the Phillies enact their own tragic ending with a final two-week tailspin which turned a 6½ game Philadelphia league-lead into a one-game pennant victory for the oncharging St. Louis Cardinals. The Redlegs bravely kept pace, finishing in a second-place dead-heat with Gene Mauch's collapsing Phillies. The biggest loser, however, was Fred Hutchinson, who died in Bradenton, Florida on November 12th at the young age of 45, wasted by the disease against which he so valiantly battled.

If hitting was the forte of Cincinnati teams throughout the 1950s and 1960s and star pitchers were but a handful in number, one of those hurlers surprisingly became – at least for brief flashes throughout the latter decade – one of the most dominant moundsmen ever to don a Cincinnati uniform. Jim Maloney featured a blazing fastball that was once timed at 99.5 mph in

One of the hardest-throwing righthanders in diamond history, Jim Maloney featured a blazing fastball that was timed at 99.5 mph in 1965 and a sterling pitching record that included double-figure victory totals for the Reds every season between 1963 and 1969. His best summers were 1963 (23-7) and 1965 (20-9), campaigns when he also hurled two of his three career no-hitters.

1965, and he was able to use it effectively enough to win in double figures each year between 1963 and 1969. Maloney enjoyed his finest season ever at 23-7 in his first full-time campaign of 1963, and once again won 20 in 1965. Yet it was rare moments of superb brilliance rather than long-haul consistency that marked Jim Maloney's schizophrenic career. He became during this period the only Reds hurler ever to throw as many as three no-hitters. In 1965 he enjoyed the rarest of distinctions, tossing two 10-inning no-hitters in the same season. The first of these two rare gems, authored against the New York Mets in June, saw 10 innings of perfection and 18 strikeouts squandered as an 11th inning homer by New Yorker Johnny Lewis resulted in a 1-0 loss. In August of the same summer the strapping righthander again tossed 10 hitless innings, this time with more positive results as the Reds bested the Cubs, 1-0. Maloney's career also featured five one-hitters and a then-league-record performance in which he would strike out eight Braves in a row on May 21, 1963. A damaged Achilles tendon and painful shoulder injury were to cut Maloney's brilliant career off by decade's end, however, and his respectable 134-84 lifetime mark was to remain as only a shadowy reminder of what might well have been.

The second half of the 1960s was marked by the departure of slugging hero Frank Robinson, the emergence of Pete Rose as a prominent hitting star, and the return of a string of lackluster second division finishes which the 1950s had featured and the earliest years of the 1960s has so far succeeded in reversing. The total collapse of Redlegs pitching in 1965 had prompted GM Bill DeWitt to peddle the popular Robinson to Baltimore for established righthanded starter Milt Pappas, yet the deal – one of the worst in club history – quickly fizzled as Pappas pitched at .500 for two seasons in Cincinnati while Robinson promptly won an American League triple crown during his very first year with the high-flying Baltimore Orioles. Pete Rose soon filled the void in the batting average department if not the power department, as he led the club in hitting all five seasons of the decade's second half, capturing two of his three career league batting titles (1968, 1969) during this otherwise barren stretch. Rose would bang out 200 or more hits in 1965, 1966 and 1968, and pace the league in runs scored in 1969 as well. Well before the opening of Riverfront Stadium and the first faint rumbles of the Big Red Machine, the legend of hometown hero Pete Rose was already alive and swinging in the old ballpark down on Findlay Avenue.

Left: *Pete Rose was already displaying his hustling flair in the infield and on the basepaths by the mid-1960s. Here Pete lunges for the errant pickoff toss of Reds hurler Jim O'Toole during Opening Day action at Crosley Field on April 12, 1965. Mack Jones is the Milwaukee runner doing some hustling of his own to get back to second base.*

Below: *Rose dives safely into third as he swipes an added base on a Vada Pinson single during 1964 action against the Pittsburgh Pirates. Pirates third baseman Bob Bailey waits in vain for the oncoming toss of rightfielder Roberto Clemente.*

7. The Big Red Machine

The National League – baseball's oldest and most stable – has known only a handful of truly dominant teams in its glorious century-plus history. Quite unlike the upstart junior circuit – which has chafed under the domination of such juggernauts as Connie Mack's Athletics of 1929-31, New York's Yankees under Miller Huggins in the 1920s and Joe McCarthy in the 1930s, Casey Stengel's Bronx Bombers throughout the 1950s and early 1960s, and the Oakland A's of the early 1970s and late 1980s – the senior circuit has been by-and-large a truly balanced league over the course of its 115-year history. There were, of course, the Honus Wagner Pirates at the turn of the century, followed by McGraw's Giants of the Mathewson era. And there were the short-lived Gas House Gang Cardinals of the late 1930s and their heavy-hitting wartime heirs paced by Mize, Musial and Slaughter in the 1940s. Standing a full head and shoulders above all other legendary teams to terrorize baseball's older league for an extended period were Roger Kahn's "Boys of Summer" Dodgers of the 1950s. Winning only one world championship in that decade, nonetheless that Brooklyn team of Jackie Robinson, Duke Snider, Roy Campanella and Pee Wee Reese holds legitimate title to the honor of the most dominant team in National League history over a full decade's play. But for a few key missing wins (for example, final day's victories in 1946, 1950, and 1951) the ballclub which Branch Rickey built would have boasted 9 championship flags in 11 summers; had they won only 19 more games over this 11-year stretch (1946-56) the Bums of Flat-

Cincinnati's own modern-day version of Murderer's Row here strikes a handsome pose in their snappy grey road uniforms. Ready for action are (l to r) Tony Perez, Johnny Bench, skipper Sparky Anderson, Joe Morgan, and Pete Rose. Anderson's debut in Redsland was a truly smashing success, as his new "Big Red Machine" ballclub streaked to 102 wins, a National League pennant, and a World Series date with the high-flying Baltimore Orioles.

bush would have garnered an unheard-of 11 straight pennants, a record not even approached by the Casey Stengel Yankees of the same era in the less-balanced American League.

When it comes to dominant senior circuit teams, however, due consideration must also be given to the Big Red Machine outfits which paraded their wares in brand spanking new Riverfront Stadium during baseball's revival decade of the 1970s. From 1970, when the hastily rebuilt team guided by new skipper George "Sparky" Anderson won its first Western Division title in only the second year of divisional play, through 1979, when largely the same outfit walked off with its sixth divisional title of the decade, the Reds won more total games and took more league titles than any other single major league ballclub. Cincinnati, in fact, piled up 953 regular season victories in this stretch (a remarkable 95 per year), thus amassing a cool .593 winning percentage (162-game schedule) for the entire decade-long era. The "Boys of Summer" Dodgers, by way of comparison, had reeled off 949 victories over the course of their own decade of domination, playing at a .614 percentage (154-game schedule) over a comparable 10-year period. No other National League franchise can boast similar marks over an equal stretch of play. Consistency of winning-style play had finally arrived at the Queen City, as it had in no previous Cincinnati baseball decade.

A fresh new era faced Reds fans when

baseball play began in 1970 in Riverfront Stadium, which would prove to be a fitting new venue for the team's drastically revised onfield image. Reds fans had said goodbye to crumbling Crosley Field on June 24, 1970 and opened modern-era Riverfront Stadium only six days later. The old ballpark, under its guises as Redland

Above: *The 1970s opened a new era in Cincinnati's long and proud diamond heritage. Not only did a new manager, a new potent offense, and a new team identity all emerge as the Queen City awoke from the turbulent 1960s, but a new showcase park was in place as well. Riverfront Stadium was a prototype for the new urban multipurpose stadiums soon to crop up everywhere in big league cities. Riverfront was the first ballpark with a "cut out" infield (with dirt only in the sliding areas).*

Left: *Here George "Sparky" Anderson strikes a confident air on the steps of the Reds' Riverfront dugout. Anderson is the most successful manager in ballclub annals.*

Above: *Was there ever a finer catcher than Johnny Bench? Few today think so, and Bench has already taken up his rightful residence among the immortals in Cooperstown. In addition to his power-hitting, Bench revolutionized his position with a bold new one-handed catching style.*

Above right: *Slugging outfielder George Foster was the last major leaguer to pound 50 homers in a single season, until Cecil Fielder of Detroit turned the trick in 1990. Foster was never known for defensive skill or hustling outfield play, but his 1977 total of 52 homers is still a Cincinnati team record.*

Field and Crosley Field, had been the site of 4543 big league games since its proud dediction day on April 11, 1912. The glitzy new ballpark destined as its replacement would be the undisputed epitome of baseball change and would usher in an entirely new era of multipurpose stadia which would soon become a special hallmark of National League cities. The Reds and their fans, therefore, were saying goodbye to a first century of baseball's oldest professional team in far more than a merely symbolic fashion. At the outset of the 1970s there was more to the Reds' altered appearance than their spiffy new carpeted stadium. Bob Howsam's administration was ushering in a modernized baseball era with a clever game plan for marketing a radically new baseball identity. And much of this new identity was credited by Howsam himself to the man selected to guide the revamped Redlegs on the field of play: George "Sparky" Anderson took over as field skipper in 1970 and remained in that post virtually the entire decade, guiding the onfield baseball strategy as well as enforcing Howsam's new clubhouse philosophies regarding the new era clean-cut Reds of the 1970s.

General manager Howsam's novel conception was a "Team of the '70s" that would earn the nickname "Big Red Machine" for its relentless winning style of play. This was a team that would excite fans all across

the nation in the "global village era" of televised baseball. And in addition to building an anticipated national following, a rekindled hometown appeal lured 21 million fans into the new Riverfront Stadium over the course of the decade. Yet for all the protestations heard from Howsam's front office about rebuilding the popularity of Reds baseball on the linchpins of Cincinnati's touted baseball traditionalism, this was a baseball franchise that now was prepared to abandon the most sacred elements of the sport's sustaining traditions. Plush-carpeted Riverfront Stadium was a certain victory for downtown urban revitalization in the Queen City and boasted a seating capacity that promised to fill the club coffers with exploding revenue; yet its circular design and plastic playing surface was clearly designed for the city's promised NFL franchise and offered little resemblance to the quaint urban ballparks that were baseball's richest heritage. Howsam's pronouncement that all Reds players would appear clean-shaven and short-haired, would don uniformly black baseball shoes, and would sport their uniform pantlegs at a prescribed height was itself reportedly a franchise reaction to the unkempt appearance and non-traditional uniform style of certain big-league teams like Charlie Finley's renegade Oakland ballclub. It was more properly assessed, however, as a

clever front-office tactic to sell a popular Reds image of "old-style baseball professionalism" to a regional Midwest audience of fans calculated to hold middle-American values and to seek leisure-time escape at the ballpark from the social upheaval of the shiftless 1970s which surrounded their everyday lives.

If Howsam's marketing strategies might be questioned, however, there could be no challenging his baseball game plan. The onfield record of the 1970s Cincinnati Reds is an unchallenged legacy of baseball perfection. Hometown fans were soon to be thrilled by 12 championships in all: six Western Division titles (1970-72-73-75-76-79), four National League flags (1970-72-75-76), and back-to-back world championships in 1975 and 1976. The Reds so dominated National League play during this span that they also walked off with league MVP honors six times in an eight-year span. Johnny Bench won the coveted award first, in 1970, and then again in 1972, when he led the NL in both homers and RBIs. Pete Rose copped the honor in 1973, when he paced the league in hitting for the third time. Joe Morgan became only the second senior circuit player to take back-to-back MVP honors when he turned the trick in the two world championship seasons. George Foster added a final MVP star to the Cincinnati bandwagon when he blasted a

club-record 52 homers and added 149 RBIs during the 1977 campaign. Foster still remains the final big league slugger to pass the rarified 50-homer plateau. And while a fifth Cincinnati star, Tony Perez, failed to match his stellar teammates with league MVP honors, he nonetheless earned an unequalled reputation for clutch hitting and superb infield play across the entire decade. Bench and Perez, in fact, ranked 1-2 in the majors in RBIs throughout the heady 1970s.

One key to the chemistry of this impressive championship team was the fact that the four luminous stars at its center – Johnny Bench, Joe Morgan, Tony Perez and Pete Rose – were men of totally different emotional makeups, personal styles, and off-field personalities; yet together they maintained a relentless common path toward victory after victory and championship after championship – as well as toward eventual Cooperstown enshrinement. In unique tandem, they provided a perfect balance of batting power, basepath speed, defense, clutch hitting, and iron-willed stability under championship pressure. Bench was the defensive leader and ranks perhaps as the game's greatest catcher. His 1989 enshrinement in Cooperstown was a foregone conclusion almost from his sensational rookie season of 1968 (15 HRs, 82 RBIs, .275 BA), if not for his all-time record

Above left: *Versatile infielder Tony Perez was an unsung hero of the Big Red Machine juggernaut. A likely Hall-of-Fame entrant, Perez now stands tied for first place with Orlando Cepeda as the all-time leading home run hitter of Latin American birth.*

Above: *Second sacker Joe Morgan has followed Johnny Bench into the sanctified halls of Cooperstown as the second Hall-of-Fame member of the Big Red Machine. Few would dispute that Morgan – despite the huge presence of Rogers Hornsby – was the best pure power-hitting second sacker in baseball history.*

home run performance as a catcher (325, a record since broken by Carlton Fisk during the 1990 season) then certainly for his stature as the man whose flashy one-handed style of receiving revolutionized the modern art of catching. The infield cornerstone was Joe Morgan, who would fittingly follow Bench into Cooperstown in 1990. Morgan had been literally stolen from the Houston Astros in a blockbuster 1971 deal which ranks as the best in franchise history, and which brought Red Machine stars Jack Billingham and Cesar Geronimo on board as well. Little Joe was the greatest power-hitting second baseman since Rogers Hornsby, extracting a remarkable 268 lifetime roundtrippers from his dimunitive 5′7″ and 150-pound frame. Rose – baseball's all-time hit leader – and Perez – the all-time home run champion among Latin American big leaguers – will themselves find Cooperstown induction only a matter of marching time, though one is now plagued by his mounting off-field problems and a lifetime ban from the sport, the other by stereotypes which will still haunt Latin American ballplayers seeking full acceptance into America's national game.

Surrounding the four superstars who were the heart and soul of the Big Red Machine stood a full contingent of sublime role players and supporting lesser stars who enjoyed outstanding performances year-in and year-out throughout the 1970s. Dave Concepcion was unrivalled by all other league shortstops of the period and teamed with Morgan to form a double play combination which won four Gold Gloves and which some consider the best of the past three decades. Ken Griffey batted .307 in nine years during his first tenure with the Reds, and patrolled the outfield with unmatched skill and speed. George Foster carried a much-deserved reputation for lackluster outfield play, yet in his halcyon period he was a true offensive giant who averaged 32 homers and 107 RBIs over a seven-year period. Cesar Geronimo anchored the other outfield spot and himself won four Gold Gloves across the brilliant decade.

The highlight seasons of this vanguard period in Reds history were the runaway pennant summers of 1975 and 1976. The 1975 team marched to a club-record 108 victories (only the 1940 and 1970 squads had previously cracked the century mark) and an unprecedented 20-game divisional lead by season's end. While Anderson's men were the only ballclub in either league to score in excess of 800 runs, they led the circuit in fielding as well. Yet they did not dominate the league's team offensive statistics this time around, as would their suc-

cessors of the following summer. Nor did they boast a single league individual hitting or pitching leader, Bench coming closest as runner-up in the league's RBI race. Great teams are often far more than the sum of their individual parts, however, and Pittsburgh's Pirates (the league's overall pacesetter in both slugging average and home run totals) could provide little challenge for Sparky Anderson's juggernaut in the playoff series which climaxed the National League pennant chase of 1975. The Reds took it in three straight, with only the final contest dragging on all the way to the final inning as a hotly contested tie game.

The World Series of 1975 has been called by many the most dramatic and well-played affair of post-season baseball history. Few would dispute that the seven-game toe-to-toe slugfest which featured five one-run decisions was far more entertaining than the 13-game difference between

Opposite: *Venezuelan Dave Concepcion was the finest shortstop in Reds history and the defensive linchpin in the Big Red machinery.*

Below: *Outfielder Cesar Geronimo was an outstanding defensive component on the five Reds division title holders, four league champions, and the 1975 and 1976 World Championship teams. The speedy Dominican came to the Reds in the very same trade which brought Joe Morgan from Houston.*

Pete Rose showcases his patented "Charlie Hustle" style of play by grabbing a foul pop fly during the final game of the 1975 World Series.

the opponents' regular season records might have forecast. The opposition was a strong Red Sox team which had outdistanced Baltimore in the AL East and then swept defending world champion Oakland in a one-sided ALCS. The Series which unfolded between these two first-time rivals was crammed with nail-biting excitement and numerous individual heroes. The evenly matched teams (despite their uneven season's records) split the first four games and then the next two. Game one featured a masterful performance by Sox starter Luis Tiant, the fiery Cuban veteran sporting a fine 18-14 season's mark, who shut out the slugging Reds with the first Series complete game effort in four years. Games three and six were both extra-inning affairs, the first falling to the Reds 6-5 in one extra bat-around and the latter to the Bosox 7-6 in 12 frames. The dramatic sixth game will live forever in baseball history through the indelible televised image of Sox catcher Carlton Fisk frantically waving fair his dramatic game-winning and Series-tying shot – barely inches fair – into the left field screen at Fenway Park. And the final game went to the very wire once again, as Joe Morgan's clutch bloop hit eventually decided it with two Reds already retired in the ninth. When reliever Will McEnaney sent down the Boston side in order in the bottom of the ninth the Reds and the long-suffering city of Cincinnati were finally able to celebrate their very first world title in 35 long and seemingly ill-starred pennant-barren years.

The following season saw the invincible Big Red Machine resist resting on its laurels as the unmatched Cincinnati powerhouse again rolled over all National League competition. For a second consecutive year the men of Sparky Anderson

Left: *Will McEnaney enjoyed a single outstanding big league season as the number two man out of the Cincinnati bullpen in 1975. With a 5-2 win-loss record and 15 saves, he posted a league second-best total of 70 game appearances. But Will's one true moment of glory came when he forced Carl Yastrzemski to sky to center for the final out of the dramatic 1975 Series.*

Below: *Joe Morgan is greeted by skipper Anderson after his extra-inning game-winning safety gave the Reds a 2-1 lead in the 1975 Series.*

Above: *An unsung star for the Reds during the Big Red Machine years, Ken Griffey batted .307 over nine seasons during his first tour of duty in Cincinnati and also challenged for the NL batting crown in both 1976 and 1977, losing by but .003 points in the 1976 campaign.*

Right: *Overshadowed on the star-studded Red Machine teams, Dan Driessen never hit quite like Ken Griffey. But the flexible Driessen did bat .301 in his rookie 1973 season and was the club's starting third baseman in 1974.*

headed the senior circuit in virtually every offensive category (Philadelphia was the only team to post a batting average within ten points of the Reds' .280 mark) and in fielding percentage as well. The final margin this time was 10 games over the Dodgers and 22 over third-place Houston in a pennant race that was virtually over before late spring planting had begun in the nation's Midwest. The Phillies (with a regular season ledger of 101-61, comparable to the Reds' 102-60) provided NLCS opposition, yet were no more an obstacle than the Pirates had been the previous year, falling in three straight games despite out-hitting the Ohioans in two of the three NLCS contests. Timely clutch hitting, especially by Foster and Bench with back-to-back game-tying homers in the third contest, brought the Redlegs back from the brink of defeat in all three games, and it was Ken Griffey's dramatic bouncing chopper off first baseman Bobby Tolan's glove which keyed a third-game three-run ninth-inning rally, bringing the Big Red Machine a delirious second pennant celebration in the late evening hours of October 12. If there were still any lonely doubters left, Griffey's charmed hit had not only dispatched the Phillies' hopes, but had also made it altogether lucid once more that these middle years of the 1970s belonged exclusively to the clean-shaven and businesslike Cincinnati Reds.

The World Series of 1976 was one of the more lopsided in Series history, a four-game whitewashing in which the Reds became simultaneously the first National League repeat world champion since McGraw's 1921-22 Giants 54 years earlier, as well as the first ballclub since the advent of divisional play to sweep both a league championship set and a World Series. In a

Series devoted to firsts, this was also the fall classic which introduced the new-fangled American League designated hitter, and in the full spirit of the one-sided affair the Reds' assigned DH Dan Driessen pounded the ball at a .357 clip, while his three Yankee counterparts (Lou Piniella, Carlos May and Elliott Maddox) were as totally ineffective at the plate as their position-playing mates. Johnny Bench emerged as the Series batting star with eight hits (four for extra bases), a lofty .533 BA and stratospheric 1.133 slugging average and two mammoth home runs in the game four clincher. Four different Reds starters (Don Gullett, Pat Zachry and Gary

Classic World Series action finds Johnny Bench diving into the stands in a futile but noble try for a pop foul during the 1976 Series finale. Bench was not only a defensive hero but the batting star as well, as the Reds cruised to their second straight World Title with a 7-2 win over the Yankees. In his finest Series performance, Bench hit a spectacular .533 in the four-game sweep, blasting two homers and leading the club with six RBIs. Both homers came in the finale and helped to overshadow an equally fine Series outing by his New York counterpart Thurman Munson, who also hit .529 for the abbreviated Fall Classic.

Right: *Don Gullett was once hailed by his manager Sparky Anderson as a sure Hall-of-Famer and the next Sandy Koufax. Such diamond immortality was not to be, however, as rotator cuff damage cut a promising career short after but nine seasons and 109 wins. Yet Gullett was a vital part of the Big Red Machine staff of the early 1970s.*

Far right: *True Hall-of-Fame status was to be the lot of Tom Seaver, however, who would register 75 of his 311 career victories in a Reds uniform.*

Nolen) claimed victories and the Reds' under-employed bullpen was hardly tested during the lopsided Series encounter in which the New Yorkers garnered only eight runs and held the lead but once (during the first three innings of game four).

The Reds remained competitive for the final three years of the decade, even taking another divisional title in 1979 after second-place finishes in the two intervening years. But the 1979 playoff series went easily to the Pirates, who had emerged as a new National League power by the end of the decade. The 1979 Western Division pennant chase had seen a close race with Houston that went right down to the season's final days. Yet despite solid seasons from such old stalwarts as George Foster (.302 BA, 30 HRs) and Johnny Bench (22 HRs, 80 RBIs), this was no longer the same Red Machine that had thrilled Riverfront Stadium fans for so long. The winds of change were blowing in Cincinnati as they were throughout the land, and the surprise departures of both Rose (as a free agent to the Phillies) and Anderson (unceremoniously dumped by an ungrateful Reds management after two pennantless years) had seemed to signal the end of the Cincinnati National League dynasty. If the depletion of the Reds' former strength was not altogether apparent during 1979 regular season play under new skipper John McNamara, it had become more tangible during the NLCS which the eventual world champion Pirates swept by scores of 5-2, 3-2

and 7-1, and in which Cincinnati bats languished at only a .215 clip.

There were a few additional highlights of this most glorious decade of Reds' history. Future Hall of Fame pitcher Tom Seaver was acquired in a blockbuster deal in 1977 and performed consistently in his Cincinnati years at the end of the decade, even if he did not match the heralded mound glories he had obtained earlier in the decade with the New York Mets. Seaver tossed a Riverfront Stadium no-hitter versus St. Louis on June 16, 1978, the only Cincinnati hitless masterpiece of the entire 1970s. And as the decade wound down in 1978, Pete Rose provided one final memorable highlight before taking his free-agent act to Philadelphia, amassing an exciting 44-game hitting streak to establish a modern-day National League milepost which has never seriously been approached since. Rose's streak, which gripped the nation's attention throughout the entire months of June and July, surpassed the twentieth-century league standard of Tommy Holmes (37 in 1945) and equalled the nineteenth-century mark established by Cooperstown immortal Wee Willie ("Hit 'em Where They Ain't") Keeler way back in 1897. As though Rose's extended hitting string were not a memorable enough farewell gift for the Cincinnati faithful who had cheered him lustily for 15 summers, the colorful Rose also stroked an historic Riverfront Stadium base hit on May 5th which made him only the 13th player in major league history with 3000 career safeties.

*Pete Rose waits in the on-deck circle (**Above**) in a familiar Riverfront scene, then takes his cuts at the plate in another (**Left**). Rose reached his career peak in the early 1970s and was the true spirit of the juggernaut Big Red Machine teams of that period. Pete's three NL batting crowns came in 1968, 1969, and 1973, and he played both the outfield and third base during this stretch of Redlegs domination in the National League baseball wars.*

8. Disappointment and Delirium at Riverfront

After a decade of glory and triumph for both the Reds and their star player Pete Rose, the bubble finally burst when four straight bridesmaid second-place seasons clouded Rose's managerial tenure between 1985 and 1988. By 1990 the Reds had their hustle back – without Charlie Hustle.

Even the most casual ballfans know that no player has banged out more base hits over the course of baseball's last century than Peter Edward Rose, the firebrand "Charlie Hustle" so permanently linked in baseball memory to the Cincinnati franchise for which he played all but a fraction of his tempestuous career. It is equally obvious, if somewhat less quantifiable, that no player has earned more press coverage in the past decade than has this same Peter Edward Rose. The 1980s, after all, was the decade in which ballooning contracts and labor disputes often drove base hits and pennant races from the front pages

of even the daily sports sections, and if Rose was indisputably the silent heart of Cincinnati baseball in the 1970s, he was the acknowledged front-and-center media attraction upon his return engagement in the Queen City during the 1980s. At each turn the Cincinnati baseball story was seemingly another momentous Rose achievement or another cataclysmic Rose revelation. And while the news was always front page stuff, it wasn't always good news, and it wasn't always strictly baseball achievements that were foremost in the public eye. Rose's failures as a field manager first disappointed the faithful in the decade's middle years. His revealed failures as a role model and baseball idol crushed the hometown fans and the nation as a whole throughout 1989. What had begun with the glorious celebration of Rose chasing Cobb at decade's dawning had dwindled to the sad image of Rose chasing his own lost stature as baseball hero by decade's dreary close.

It didn't begin this way at the outset of the 1980s, however, as the Pete Rose story was still strictly baseball milestones at the dawn of the decade. The early years of the 1980s were, in fact, the years that Pete Rose was strangely absent from Riverfront Stadium, though hardly absent as headline grabber from the larger baseball scene. Pete was now chasing down Ty Cobb in the rival city of Philadelphia. Having mounted the last serious threat to DiMaggio's legendary hit-streak and having also become the youngest player ever to reach the 3000-hit milestone at the outset of the 1978 campaign, Rose turned to the lure of the free agent market once the Reds allowed his contract to lapse at the conclusion of that same season. In the fierce bidding war that followed, Rose had signed on for a then-staggering four-year $3.2 million contract with the rebuilding Phillies. And the events that surrounded his departure from his home town were only the first painful episode in the reckless dismantling of the team that had so dominated the previous baseball decade.

Rose had justifiably grabbed a piece of

the free-agent bonanza which now awaited high-profile superstars and which was apparently not to be offered by the frugal Reds who had exploited his talents for 15 previous summers. And Rose was not the only star who was now cast aside or allowed to drift away by the front office regime of new club president Dick Wagner. Tony Perez was first to be unloaded, to Montreal on the heels of the 1976 World Series triumph, for mainstream pitchers Woodie Fryman and Dale Murray. When Joe Morgan's own free agent status arrived in January 1980 the incomparable second sacker was allowed to drift unchallenged back to Houston where his career had started. So too went George Foster, dealt to the Mets for two journeyman pitchers and undistinguished catcher Alex Treviño before the opening of the 1982 season. Even such lesser figures as Ken

Griffey (sent to the Yankees for minor league hurlers Fred Toliver and Bryan Ryder in November 1981) and Cesar Geronimo (peddled to Kansas City in January 1981) were allowed to escape to greener pastures in more free-spending baseball organizations.

But if the 1980s were to be a period of decline and disappointment at Riverfront Stadium, this was not yet altogether evident to the local partisans at the outset of the 1981 season, no matter how many new and untried faces (like Ron Oester at second, Ray Knight at third, Dan Driessen at first and Dave Collins in right) had replaced the popular old guard of Morgan, Rose, Perez and Griffey. At least the decline was not to be immediately evident, though the element of disappointment was every bit rampant enough and bitter enough from

Far left: *Slightly built Ed Milner was one of the swiftest and most adept center fielders of the early 1980s and stole 41 bases for the Reds in 1983.*

Left: *Ron Oester became the Reds' starting second baseman in 1980. Injury cut his playing time by 1987, but Oester battled back and was still a role player with the Reds in 1990, scoring the pennant-clinching run in the tense NLCS Game 6 victory over the Pirates.*

Far left: *Barry Larkin was the Reds' first pick in the June 1985 amateur draft and is now the heir-apparent to Dave Concepcion's shortstop position. He hit .340 for the first half-season in 1989 before injury ended a run at the hit crown.*

Left: *John Franco emerged as a bullpen stopper for the Reds in 1986-89, recording totals of 29, 32, and 39 saves in the first three years of that stretch.*

Rotund slugger Dave Parker brought a troubled past from Pittsburgh when he returned to his hometown Reds in 1984. A perennial all-star throughout the 1970s in the Steel City, Parker's star tarnished in the early 1980s as rumors of drug use combined with his slipping on-field play. His return to Cincinnati brought career renewal, however, and in 1985 the big lefty outfielder enjoyed another banner year with a .312 BA, 34 homers, and a league-best 125 RBI total. Parker was traded to the A's at the end of 1987.

the first season of the new decade. The Reds battled valiantly for a pennant in 1980 but didn't quite make it down the stretch, finishing three games behind Houston and LA in a tightly-contested league race which saw the issue between Los Angeles and Houston decided in a dramatic playoff contest, forced by the Dodgers' sweep of the Astros in the season's final three games. Most frustrating for Cincinnati fans, meanwhile, was the fact that while the locals came up with just too little hitting to stay glued to the Dodgers and Astros, in the meantime Pete Rose was now leading Philadelphia to a pennant and world title with his consistent bat and stellar first base play. There were, at the same time, few big-name stars apparent in Cincinnati. Dave Collins (.303) was the only regular to hit at .300; Foster (25) and Bench (24) provided the home run power but were far in arrears of the league leaders.

Yet the makings of a good team were still there, and the 1981 season promised to be proof that the Big Red Machine had sputtered but was hardly dead in the water. It

was also that 1981 season, however, that was soon enough to prove perhaps the most frustrating in the long and storied history of Cincinnati baseball. This was, in fact, to be arguably the most bizarre season in all of baseball history, and it was certainly the most unfair. Unable to reach agreement with ownership over the issue of free agent compensation, the Players' Association called a halt to the season's action on June 12, launching a 50-day labor action which became the longest strike in the history of organized sport and wiped out 714 big league games. Cincinnati had boasted baseball's best record (66-42, .611 Pct) that year, from opening gun to final bell. Yet the unpopular players' strike did what the rest of the league could not, altogether derailing the Reds' own cherished pennant plans. A makeshift and illogical jerry-built playoff system, driven by the owners' and players' apparent joint greed for television dollars, dictated once play resumed on August 1 that the season would (after the fact) be divided into two independent segments. Half-season winners would meet in an additional set of lucrative revenue-producing playoffs. The result was that the team with baseball's best record would not participate, while one team (the New York Yankees) that finished in sixth place during the post-strike segment would somehow be a playoff guest. The Reds – who remained one-half game behind the Dodgers when Strike Day abruptly concluded "Season One" and then trailed Houston by a game-and-a-half at the close of the makeshift "Season Two" – found little true satisfaction and reaped little fan promotional payoff by hoisting their own flag (proclaiming their ownership of baseball's best record) at season's end on the final weekend of play in Riverfront Stadium.

There were some bright stories in 1981, though, and the brightest was perhaps Tom Seaver. In this senseless season, Seaver became only the fifth hurler in history to reach the milestone of 3000 career strikeouts, surpassing that number in an April 18 game with St. Louis, ironically only 11 days before veteran Steve Carlton of Philadelphia's Phillies also reached the charmed 3000 circle. For Seaver, who led the strike-shortened campaign in victories (14) and winning percentage (.875), 1981 was a final milestone season preceding a less fortunate sub-.500 swansong in Cincinnati the following summer.

Things were soon to get worse before they got much better, and the three summers following the bizarre 1981 campaign were a period of change, turmoil and plummeting league standings in Redsland. The altogether forgettable 1982 campaign brought with it the only Reds ballclub ever to lose as many as 100 league contests. And there were three consecutive embarrassing seasons in the second division during this stretch, a period of decline which saw the front office test first Russ Nixon and then Vern Rapp as possible successors to ousted skipper John McNamara. Meanwhile, Rose had been joined in Philadelphia by Morgan and Perez, and the aged Red Machine was now grinding out yet another pennant in the City of Brotherly Love, sweeping to a 1983 National League flag and World Series date with Baltimore which was Philly's second in four summers.

In the midst of this dramatic and dispiriting downturn some familiar faces unexpectedly returned to Riverfront Stadium and thus temporarily buoyed sagging hometown spirits. The first was Bob Howsam, back on board as club president after the dismissal of unpopular Dick Wagner, Howsam's replacement in 1978 and target of fan ire for his role in dismantling the fabled Big Red Machine. Howsam's first and most popular act was to bring Rose back home to Cincinnati. Saddled with a burdensome salary, aging legs, and an expired Philadelphia contract, Pete had moved on to Montreal in spring 1984, where

Left: *The Reds made Jack Armstrong their top amateur draft pick in 1987, and the big righthander began to show promise of a bright future during the 1990 pennant-winning season. Armstrong was 2-3 as a starter for the disappointing 1989 Reds, but has yet to show his minor league potential which saw him throw a classy 1988 no-hitter against Indianapolis while hurler for the AAA Nashville Sounds American Association ballclub.*

Left: *Mario Soto was a hard-throwing Dominican righthander whose 100-92 11-year career mark with the Reds enabled him to become only the tenth Latin American pitcher to earn as many as 100 big league victories. Soto's best season was recorded in 1984, when his 18-7 mark established the top winning percentage (.720) that season in the senior circuit.*

he promptly stroked his 4000th career hit, a day before his 44th birthday and exactly 21 years from the date of his first big league hit. In August – one of the most glorious stretches of Reds history – Rose was traded back to his hometown Reds, installed as player-manager, and responded with a .365 BA down the final 26-game stretch of the season. While Pete Rose was again the major news on the field in 1984, the front office also underwent another significant change, as new owner Marge Schott came on board with the reputation of a hard-nosed businesswoman who let her heart rule in baseball matters but her pocketbook rule all else. The baseball marriage of Pete Rose and Marge Schott was to be a rocky one from the beginning, just as was the marriage of the unpredictable and brassy auto dealer and the bulk of Cincinnati's fans. Reds supporters soon ran the gamut of emotions with their new owner – excited by her free-spending acquisition of expensive ballplayers like Buddy Bell, Bo Diaz and Bill Gullickson and exasperated by her ubiquitous Saint Bernard Schottzie, her meddling with baseball matters best left to the baseball people of the organization, and most of all her dismantling of the Reds farm system under the direction of Branch Rickey III.

The season of 1985 was indisputably the "Year of Pete Rose" as the nation's summer seemingly revolved entirely around Rose's unwinding chase after the ghost of Ty Cobb. Tension mounted as Rose approached the vaunted record in a September weekend series in Chicago. Player-manager Rose had intended to sit out the September 8 game at Wrigley Field – still two hits shy of Cobb – and assure the record-setting moment for the home crowds in Cincinnati. But a last minute Cubs pitching change (righty Reggie Patterson for the announced lefty Steve Trout) had the win-at-all-costs Rose back in the lineup and owner Marge

Right: *Owner Marge Schott poses with the ever-present mascot Schottsie, a Riverfront Stadium fixture throughout the 1980s.*

Below: *Pete Rose writes his name in the record book for all time as he here singles off San Diego Padres hurler Eric Show to set a new career hit record at 4192, ending the long quest after Ty Cobb's once seemingly unapproachable 60-year-old standard.*

Schott scurrying to the Windy City in a hastily chartered jet to be on hand just in case. A Rose single in the first inning brought Chicago pandemonium and another in the fifth brought not ony a tie with the immortal Cobb but horror in the Reds front office back in Cincinnati. Reds management breathed a gasp of relief, however, when the record-shattering hit did not materialize during Rose's final two at-bats in Chicago, then braced for both a gate bonanza and an inevitable joyous celebration in the hometown park the following week. After almost two seasons of non-stop media glare, the dramatic chase of Cobb came to its fitting emotional conclusion in Riverfront Stadium on the night of September 11, as the irrepressible Rose lined a single to left off Padres starter Eric Show to pass Cobb in the official record books, if not also in the game's unofficial yet immortal halls of legend.

With the coveted hit-record finally in his pocket, Rose turned to full-time managing after a final summer of part-time play in 1986. The next few seasons would bring repeated disappointments, however, as Rose's teams always seemed predestined to be bridesmaids rather than brides. Picked as the divisional shoo-in in March of 1987 and 1988, two more somewhat lackluster second-place finishes made it four straight runner-up slots for Rose since assuming full-time control in 1985. None of these

races actually went down to the wire – the closest finish was the 5.5-game debit to the Dodgers in 1985 – and the local faithful were beginning to wonder aloud if the management-ownership team of Rose-Schott had the wherewithal to return winning baseball to the ballpark which had enjoyed such unbroken successes during its maiden decade.

There were some limited individual heroics in this stretch, to be sure. Tom Browning's rain-delayed perfect game (1-0 versus Los Angeles) at Riverfront on September 16, 1988 was the first "perfect ace" in Reds history and the first as well in 23 years of National League play. Slender yet powerful Eric Davis emerged by 1987 (37 homers, National League All-Star selection, Gold Glove winner) as a new superstar and one of the finest young slugging outfielders of the decade. But there was also a distinctly bitter taste after each season, when so much had been forecast and so little had been actually won. As the Reds headed into the portentous 1989 season, with another divisional crown already being predicted by many pre-season pundits, Pete Rose's managerial skills – especially his ability to use his overtaxed bullpen effectively and to shuffle his starting mount rotation properly – was subject for lengthy serious debate among casual fans and "baseball experts" alike.

But all this was lost with the dramatic

Above left: *Eric Davis displays the free-swinging style that made him one of the NL's most feared hitters in the second half of the 1980s.*

Above: *Tom Browning broke into the big-time with a bang in 1985, as the first rookie to win 20 games since Bob Grim turned the trick for the New York Yankees in 1954. Then on September 16, 1988, Browning achieved instant immortality with a perfect game masterpiece against the Dodgers at Riverfront Stadium.*

Post-season mound hero Danny Jackson fires away at the Pirates in the first inning of Game 6 of the NLCS. Injuries slowed Jackson throughout the 1990 campaign but seemingly had little effect on the crafty lefthander's October mound clinic. Despite a mediocre 3.61 ERA and disappointing 6-6 standard throughout 1990 regular season action, it was Danny Jackson who clinched the National League title with a nifty one-hit playoff effort against the Pittsburghers, and who also kept the Reds close enough in the early innings of Series Game 2 to allow a comeback extra-inning win that would soon launch Cincinnati on an unexpected Series sweep of the mighty Oakland Athletics.

events of 1989, one of baseball's worst public relations seasons since the devastating Black Sox summer of 1919, which also ironically had involved the baseball-saturated but seemingly ill-blessed town of Cincinnati. News of a Commissioner's investigation of Rose for allegedly wagering on baseball games first surfaced during spring training. From the moment the story first dramatically broke, the Reds and their popular manager were the focus of a relentless media glare. Little chance remained for a successful National League season with Rose at the helm, as attention was too much distracted from the total team concentration necessary for winning a league pennant. Rose refused to step down, however, and maintained his innocence of all charges as well as his freedom from rumored gambling addiction. Marge Schott steadfastly refused to remove her beleaguered manager, obviously aware of his remaining untarnished local popularity. The season, quite predictably, drifted away in the process as the Reds early fell far off the pace and maintained a season's edge on only the hapless Braves from Atlanta. Finally, the dramatic mid-summer announcement was made by Commissioner A. Barlett Giamatti that Rose had agreed to a lifetime suspension from the national pastime. Days later Rose shocked the remaining faithful and his still considerable bands of true believers by admitting his long-standing gambling addiction. Coach Tommy Helms was named interim manager and the season was played out under the darkest of palls.

If the events of the tragic 1989 season were not shocking enough, popular Commissioner Giamatti suffered a fatal heart attack only one week after issuing his landmark edict against Rose. For Pete Rose himself the Hall of Fame was now no longer a certainty. Yet this seemed a small enough matter as deep personal problems mounted for baseball's tarnished hero, now facing income tax evasion charges stemming from hidden track winnings and unreported dealings in baseball memorabilia. Meanwhile the nation's fans continued to debate whether or not Rose – baseball's greatest hero of the post-Vietnam era but also now a convicted felon – still merited their nod for Hall of Fame enshrinement in Cooperstown.

While Rose, the admitted gambler and accused tax felon, would not fade from the headlines at the end of a decade which had seen contracts, labor actions, and courtroom drama repeatedly overshadow diamond play, baseball was indeed still being played – often in most dramatic fashion – in Riverfront Stadium and throughout other league cities. The summer of 1990 seemed to bring winds of fresh hope, with the Rose scandal largely behind the Reds' beleaguered organization and a new management team now on board. Ex-Yankee skipper Lou Piniella had taken over the reins from interim skipper Helms and Piniella's charges started remarkably fast, sprinting to a double-digit lead over the Giants and Dodgers in the season's first six weeks and maintaining a 10-game edge and .630 winning percentage as late in the season as July 1.

By mid-season the Reds were fading badly, however, and a disastrous road-trip losing skein in early August allowed the Dodgers and Giants to creep back into the race. And by mid-summer the specter of Pete Rose was once again the dominant Cincinnati baseball story, as Rose was convicted by a federal judge of income tax evasion and sentenced to serve prison time for his several misdeeds. Even the fast start by Piniella's exciting 1990 Reds team was seemingly not enough to compete with Rose for the nation's baseball headlines; and when Piniella's team had finally charged back onto the front page, it was a disastrous Cincinnati tailspin and not a runaway pennant race which was the talk of the nation's baseball fans. Pete Rose and the Reds of the dynamic 1980s no longer wore the glamorous image they had once sported a decade earlier. But no one following baseball religiously could accuse these two Cincinnati baseball institutions of being the slightest bit dull either.

By the end of the 1990 season the Cincin-

Left: *Leader of Cincinnati's talented and much-touted "Nasty Boys" bullpen corps, fastballing reliever Rob Dibble was one of a host of post-season unsung heroes for the triumphant 1990 Reds. Here hard-throwing Dibble works his magic against the Pirates during a Cincinnati 6-3 win in NLCS Game 3 at Three Rivers Stadium.*

nati Reds had indeed proved to be a team full of surprises. The grandest surprise had been the fast start the team enjoyed, one which created shock waves throughout the Western Division from which the Reds' divisional rivals could never recover. An additional surprise was the team's ability to hang on down the season's final stretch, despite a horrendous slump in starting pitching which the league's many doom-sayers had predicted all along. The Reds were barely a .500 ballclub after June 1, but the men of Lou Piniella never folded completely when a National League crown was on the line in the month of September, something that couldn't be said of Cincinnati teams during the previous four campaigns. The heroes on the young club were many. Most attention in the media went to the "Nasty Boys" bullpen, and much of this was merited (Randy Myers registered 31 saves and Rob Dibble added 11). Chris Sabo (club home run leader with 25) enjoyed a fine if not spectacular season, as did Barry Larkin (the batting average pacesetter at .301) and Eric Davis (24 homers and a club-best 86 RBIs). Newcomer Hal Morris contributed when sparingly used, hitting .340 in 309 at bats spread over 107 games. Together they earned a divisional title by five games over the late-season charge of the revitalized Dodgers.

If it was not entirely certain for a while during the final months of summer whether or not a decade of disappointment had indeed finally ended in Riverfront, there was little doubt or much concern once the post-season finally arrived. On the surface at

Left: *Had there not been so many 1990 post-season heroes for the team-oriented Reds of manager Lou Piniella, Chris Sabo might well have been tabbed as 1990 World Series MVP. Sabo hit .563 for the four-game set, provided outstanding third-base play, and even crushed two homers in the Game 3 rout of favored Oakland. Sabo is captured here in early season plate action against the rival New York Mets in Shea Stadium.*

least, the Reds and their Eastern Division rivals from Pittsburgh were evenly matched in all phases of the game. The Pirates might have been granted the edge in starting pitching (as the Reds had no dominant starter to match the Pirates' Cy Young shoo-in Doug Drabek), but the bullpen clearly belonged to the Reds (with Dibble, Myers, and Norm Charlton considered the most intimidating closers in the league). And the NLCS playoff week which unfolded at season's end followed exactly true to this form. The Pirates jumped out on top in a nail-biter, a 4-3 triumph at Riverfront brought on by Eric Davis's misplay of an Andy Van Slyke fly-ball double in the seventh frame. The Reds then swept three straight, the final two coming in Pittsburgh's Three Rivers Stadium behind the starting pitching of Danny Jackson and Jose Rijo. The Pirates bounced back with a needed win (3-2, behind ace Doug Drabek in the final Pirate home game) to return the Series to the Queen City. But then the revived Cincinnati pitching again held sway in the sixth game, as Danny Jackson spun pure magic at the Pittsburghers. Jackson pitched no-hit ball until Carmelo Martinez poked a lone run-producing double in the fifth, and then Myers and Charlton came on to no-hit the dormant Pittsburgh bats over the final three frames. When Glenn Braggs reached above the barrier to nab Carmelo Martinez's second long drive to right in the final inning, the Reds had at long last won their ninth National League crown, their first in the fourteen long and often bitterly disappointing seasons which had transpired since the last hurrah of the Big Red Machine way back in 1976.

If the NCLS had been almost too close to call in advance, all the experts had easily pegged the Oakland Athletics as the 1990 World Series victors. But the oft-overlooked Cincinnati team of skipper Lou Piniella had saved the grandest surprise for last, and that surprise erupted in full view of the nation's television screens in the very first inning of the very first Series game. Eric Davis, in the throes of a season-ending and injury-induced slump, blasted a resounding homer off invincible Oakland starter Stewart (winner of six straight postseason outings) and it was suddenly apparent that the hometown Reds were fully capable of doing some impressive hitting and pitching of their own. The Reds went on to win 7-0 in Game One. Game Two gave every appearance of a quick rebound for Oakland, but in the end the Reds' bullpen was better than its junior circuit counterpart, and the Cincinnati team earned a tight 5-4 10-inning heart-stopper for a two-game Riverfront sweep.

Oakland's once-mighty Athletics limped back to the West Coast in a state of shock and disbelief. Their own dreams of a quick Series sweep had been rudely turned upside-down, and it was suddenly Oakland who was facing imminent elimination. The Game Three change of venue would bring renewed hope to West Coast fans, but nothing of the kind was to be. While Billy Hatcher had burned up Oakland pitching in the first two games, it was Chris Sabo who took over in Game Three. One mighty inning again sent Oakland reeling as the steamrolling Reds jumped on a third disappointing Oakland starter, Mike Moore, for seven runs and seven hits during a landslide third frame. By the time Game Four arrived the nation's fans and the sporting press had been equally convinced that a miraculous upset was unfolding before their very eyes. Jose Rijo was at his career best and did not allow even a hit after the first inning. The Athletics had scored first in the initial frame, on a fly-ball double (lofted by Willie McGee and dropped by a diving Eric Davis, who suffered a severe kidney bruise on the play and had to be removed from further competition) and a following single by Carney Lansford; and then Oakland bats went fully dormant once more. When the Reds posted two lonely tallies in the eighth frame, it was all that the dominant Rijo needed. With help from Randy Myers in the ninth, the Reds starter cruised to his second Series victory and to a Fall Classic MVP award as well. And only five days after it had opened, the 1990 World Series belonged to the Cincinnati Reds.

The Reds' surprising 1990 pennant and World Series victories were earned by a total team effort. Thus as winter 1990 set in across the Queen City, Redlegs fans were once again dreaming the most pleasant of dreams – about a new Cincinnati baseball dynasty.

The Reds' "Mr. Cool," Billy Hatcher, blows a bubble while getting an intentional walk in the dramatic ninth inning of hard-fought Series Game 2 at Riverfront Stadium. The Oakland brain trust had good enough reason for walking the dangerous Hatcher, who had just set a new World Series standard with seven straight previous base hits. Hatcher's .750 BA for the four-game Series would also stand as a new record, outpacing the .625 mark of Babe Ruth set in 1928.

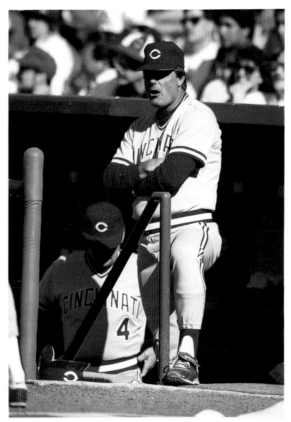

Far left: *Reds' "Dominican Dandy" Jose Rijo fires the first pitch of the 1990 World Series to Oakland's Rickey Henderson. Five days later Rijo would reign as Series MVP.*

Left: *Lou Piniella was the man of the hour on the Cincinnati bench as the Reds cruised to their fifth World Championship in club history.*

Below: *The long-awaited celebration begins on the West Coast as the Midwest Reds take their first World Series title since 1976.*

Reds TEAM RECORDS

YEAR-BY-YEAR REDS STANDINGS

Year	Pos.	Record	Margin	Manager
National League				
1876	8	9-56	−42½	Charlie Gould
1877	6	15-42	−25½	Lipman Pike
				Bob Addy
1878	2	37-23	− 4	Cal McVey
1879	5	38-36	−14	Cal McVey
				Deacon White
1880	8	21-59	−44	John Clapp
1881	No team			
American Association				
1882	1	55-25	+11½	Pop Snyder
1883	3	61-37	− 5	Pop Snyder
1884	5	68-41	− 8	Pop Snyder
				Will White
1885	2	63-49	−16	O.P. Caylor
1886	5	65-73	−27½	O.P. Caylor
1887	2	81-54	−14	Gus Schmelz
1888	4	80-54	−11½	Gus Schmelz
1889	4	76-63	−18	Gus Schmelz
National League				
1890	4	78-55	−10½	Tom Loftus
1891	7	56-81	−30½	Tom Loftus
1892	5	82-68	−20	Charles Comiskey
1893	6	65-63	−20½	Charles Comiskey
1894	10	54-75	−35	Charles Comiskey
1895	8	66-64	−21	Buck Ewing
1896	3	77-50	−12	Buck Ewing
1897	4	76-56	−17	Buck Ewing
1898	3	92-60	−11½	Buck Ewing
1899	6	83-67	−19	Buck Ewing
1900	7	62-77	−21½	Bob Allen
1901	8	52-87	−38	Bid McPhee
1902	4	70-70	−33½	Bid McPhee
				Frank Bancroft
				Joe Kelley
1903	4	74-65	−16½	Joe Kelley
1904	3	88-65	−18	Joe Kelley
1905	5	79-74	−26	Joe Kelley
1906	6	64-87	−51½	Ned Hanlon
1907	6	66-87	−41½	Ned Hanlon
1908	5	73-81	−26	John Ganzel
1909	4	77-76	−33½	Clark Griffith
1910	5	75-79	−29	Clark Griffith
1911	6	70-83	−29	Clark Griffith
1912	4	75-78	−29	Hank O'Day
1913	7	64-89	−37½	Joe Tinker
1914	8	60-94	−34½	Buck Herzog
1915	7	71-83	−20	Buck Herzog
1916	7	60-93	−33½	Buck Herzog
				Ivy Wingo
				Christy Mathewson
1917	4	78-76	−20	Christy Mathewson
1918	3	68-60	−15½	Christy Mathewson
				Heinie Groh
1919	**1**	96-44	+ 9	Pat Moran
1920	3	82-71	−10½	Pat Moran
1921	6	70-83	−24	Pat Moran
1922	2	86-68	− 7	Pat Moran
1923	2	91-63	− 4½	Pat Moran
1924	4	83-70	−10	Jack Hendricks
1925	3	80-73	−15	Jack Hendricks
1926	2	87-67	− 2	Jack Hendricks
1927	5	75-78	−18½	Jack Hendricks
1928	5	78-74	−16	Jack Hendricks
1929	7	66-88	−33	Jack Hendricks
1930	7	59-95	−33	Dan Howley
1931	8	58-96	−43	Dan Howley
1932	8	60-94	−30	Dan Howley
1933	8	58-94	−33	Donie Bush
1934	8	52-99	−42	Bob O'Farrell
				Burt Shotton
				Chuck Dressen
1935	6	68-85	−31½	Chuck Dressen
1936	5	74-80	−18	Chuck Dressen
1937	8	56-98	−40	Chuck Dressen
				Bobby Wallace
1938	4	82-68	− 6	Bill McKechnie
1939	**1**	97-57	+ 4½	Bill McKechnie
1940	**1**	100-53	+12	Bill McKechnie
1941	3	88-66	−12	Bill McKechnie
1942	4	76-76	−29	Bill McKechnie
1943	2	87-67	−18	Bill McKechnie
1944	3	89-65	−16	Bill McKechnie
1945	7	61-93	−37	Bill McKechnie
1946	6	67-87	−30	Bill McKechnie
1947	5	73-81	−21	Johnny Neun
1948	7	64-89	−27	Johnny Neun
				Bucky Walters
1949	7	62-92	−35	Bucky Walters
1950	6	66-87	−24½	Luke Sewell
1951	6	68-86	−28½	Luke Sewell
1952	6	69-85	−27½	Luke Sewell
				Earle Brucker
				Rogers Hornsby
1953	6	68-86	−37	Rogers Hornsby
				Buster Mills
1954	5	74-80	−23	Birdie Tebbetts
1955	5	75-79	−23½	Birdie Tebbetts
1956	3	91-63	− 2	Birdie Tebbetts
1957	4	80-74	−15	Birdie Tebbetts
1958	4	76-78	−16	Birdie Tebbetts
				Jimmy Dykes
1959	5	74-80	−13	Mayo Smith
				Fred Hutchinson
1960	6	67-87	−28	Fred Hutchinson
1961	**1**	93-61	+ 4	Fred Hutchinson
1962	3	98-64	− 3½	Fred Hutchinson
1963	5	86-76	−13	Fred Hutchinson
1964	2	92-70	− 1	Fred Hutchinson
				Dick Sisler
1965	4	89-73	− 8	Dick Sisler
1966	7	76-84	−18	Don Heffner
				Dave Bristol
1967	4	87-75	−14½	Dave Bristol
1968	4	83-79	−14	Dave Bristol
National League (Western Division)				
1969	3	89-73	− 4	Dave Bristol
1970	**1**	102-60	+14½	Sparky Anderson
1971	4	79-83	−11	Sparky Anderson
1972	**1**	95-59	+10½	Sparky Anderson
1973	**1**	99-63	+ 3½	Sparky Anderson
1974	2	98-64	− 4	Sparky Anderson
1975	**1**	108-54	+20	Sparky Anderson
1976	1	102-60	+10	Sparky Anderson
1977	2	88-74	−10	Sparky Anderson
1978	2	92-69	− 2½	Sparky Anderson
1979	**1**	90-71	+ 1½	John McNamara
1980	3	89-73	− 3½	John McNamara
1981**	1	66-42	+ 4	John McNamara
1982	6	61-101	−28	John McNamara
				Russ Nixon
1983	6	74-88	−17	Russ Nixon
1984	5	70-92	−22	Vern Rapp
				Pete Rose
1985	2	89-72	− 5½	Pete Rose
1986	2	86-76	−10	Pete Rose
1987	2	84-78	− 6	Pete Rose
1988	2	87-74	− 7	Pete Rose
1989	5	75-87	−17	Pete Rose
				Tommy Helms
1990	**1**	91-71	+ 5	Lou Piniella

**Did not qualify for League Championship Series under split-season playoff format

HALL OF FAMERS

Name	Position	Year Elected
Christy Mathewson	P*	1936
George Wright	Manager	1937
Charles Comiskey	P*	1939
Buck Ewing	C–1B	1939
Candy Cummings	P	1939
Charles Radbourne	P	1939
Rogers Hornsby	2B*	1942
Mike "King" Kelly	C	1945
Clark Griffith	Manager**	1946
Joe Tinker	SS	1946
Three-Finger Brown	P	1949
Harry Heilmann	OF	1952
Al Simmons	OF	1953
Bobby Wallace	SS	1953
Harry Wright	Manager	1953
Dazzy Vance	P	1955
Sam Crawford	OF	1957
Bill McKechnie	Manager	1962
Edd Roush	OF	1962
Eppa Rixey	P	1963
Miller Huggins	Manager***	1964
Lloyd Waner	OF	1967
Kiki Cuyler	OF	1968
Jesse Haines	P	1970
Jake Beckley	1B	1971
Chick Hafey	OF	1971
Joe Kelley	OF	1971
Rube Marquard	P	1971
George Kelly	1B	1973
Jim Bottomley	1B	1974
Amos Rusie	P	1977
Frank Robinson	OF	1982
Johnny Bench	C	1989
Joe Morgan	2B	1990

*Manager while with Cincinnati Reds
**Pitcher while with Cincinnati Reds
***Infielder while with Cincinnati Reds

ALL-TIME REDS CAREER BATTING LEADERS

Games Played	Pete Rose	2722
At Bats	Pete Rose	10,934
Runs Scored	Pete Rose	1741
Hits	Pete Rose	3358
Batting Average (300 or more games)	Cy Seymour	.333
Doubles	Pete Rose	601
Triples	Edd Roush	153
Home Runs	Johnny Bench	389
Extra Base Hits	Pete Rose	868
Runs Batted in	Johnny Bench	1376
Stolen Bases	Joe Morgan	406
Total Bases	Pete Rose	4645

ALL-TIME REDS CAREER PITCHING LEADERS

Innings Pitched	Eppa Rixey	2890
ERA (1000+ Inns)	Bob Ewing	2.37
Wins	Eppa Rixey	179
Strikeouts	Jim Maloney	1592
Bases on Balls	Johnny Vander Meer	1072
Games	Pedro Borbon	531
Shutouts	Bucky Walters	32
Saves	John Franco	148
Games Started	Eppa Rixey	356
Complete Games	Noodles Hahn	207

SINGLE-SEASON REDS BATTING RECORDS

Batting Average (350 ABs)	Cy Seymour	.377	1905
At Bats	Pete Rose	680	1973
Home Runs	George Foster	52	1977
Runs Batted In	George Foster	149	1977
Hits	Pete Rose	230	1973
Runs	Frank Robinson	134	1962
Singles	Pete Rose	181	1973
Doubles	Frank Robinson	51	1962
	Pete Rose	51	1978
Triples	Sam Crawford	23	1902
Slugging Pct.	Ted Kluszewski	.642	1954
Extra Base Hits	Frank Robinson	92	1962
Stolen Bases	Bob Bescher	81	1911
Pinch Hits	Jerry Lynch	19	1960 1961
Most Strikeouts	Lee May	142	1969
Bases on Balls	Joe Morgan	132	1975
Total Bases	George Foster	388	1977
Hitting Streak	Pete Rose	44	1978

SINGLE-SEASON REDS PITCHING RECORDS

ERA (150 Inns)	Fred Toney	1.75	1915
Wins	Dolf Luque	27	1923
	Bucky Walters	27	1939
Losses	Paul Derringer	25	1933
Winning Pct. (10 decisions)	Tom Seaver	.875	1981
Winning Pct. (20 victories)	Bob Purkey	.831	1962
Strikeouts	Mario Soto	274	1982
Saves	John Franco	39	1988
Game Appearances	Wayne Granger	90	1969
Complete Games	Noodles Hahn	41	1901
Games Started	Noodles Hahn	42	1901
Innings Pitched	Noodles Hahn	375	1901
Shutouts	Jack Billingham	7	1973
	Rod Eller	7	1919
	Fred Toney	7	1917
	Jake Weimer	7	1906

REDS POST-SEASON RECORD

Playoffs (NLCS)

Year	Opponent	Wins-Losses
1970	**Pittsburgh Pirates**	**3-0**
1972	**Pittsburgh Pirates**	**3-2**
1973	New York Mets	2-3
1975	**Pittsburgh Pirates**	**3-0**
1976	**Philadelphia Phillies**	**3-0**
1979	Pittsburgh Pirates	0-3
1990	**Pittsburgh Pirates**	**4-2**

World Series

Year	Opponent	Wins-Losses
1919	**Chicago White Sox**	**5-3**
1939	New York Yankees	0-4
1940	**Detroit Tigers**	**4-3**
1961	New York Yankees	1-4
1970	Baltimore Orioles	1-4
1972	Oakland Athletics	3-4
1975	**Boston Red Sox**	**4-3**
1976	**New York Yankees**	**4-0**
1990	**Oakland Athletics**	**4-0**

Index